PLEASE TRY YOUR CALL AGAIN LATER

My Journey Through Customer Service Hell for Pandemic Relief

"The Notorious Banker"
James Baca

This book is dedicated to every person who has gone through hell dealing with their state, bank, or a customer service representative for help during the COVID-19 Pandemic. Millions of people have been impacted by the fallout from COVID-19, and millions have been helped. But for the rest of the people stuck in an endless loop of muzak, untrained customer service reps, and miles of red tape, this one's for you.

I sincerely hope you have good health, physically, mentally, and fiscally, and that you have someone helping you get back on track through these "unprecedented times." (Don't you just love that phrase?)

This world can be unforgiving to those who don't have any money nor the means to get any. Working for a major bank for years, I see what drove people in power, and I hope that by some luck, this book gets me the assistance I so greatly deserve and desire. Still, I hope it empowers you to work hard to get what is rightfully yours, by law, and by hard work and determination.

Give 'em Hell!

Copyright 2021 – The Notorious Banker, LLC

CONTENTS

Title Page
Dedication
A Brief Note
Contact Info
How We Got Here
My 9-Month Near-Fruitless Journey for Help — 18
How Customer Service Has Changed Since COVID-19 — 43
An Open Letter to the Haters — 53
Donating Plasma and the Battle To Stay Solvent While Waiting -- How I Have Always Been Resilient — 63
Seeing How States and Banks Systematically Kept People from Help — 78
My State: Not Winning — 94
Giving Back - My Mission Going Forward — 103
"Trampoline Money" - My Detailed Plans for My Unemployment Benefits — 118
Finally… — 162
But Wait, There's More! — 171
Thank You — 185
About The Author — 189

A BRIEF NOTE

I just wanted to write this note briefly before we get into the book. Writing is my love and my passion. Sometimes the things I type out don't reflect how it's written in my head. Every writer can attest to this. It can make thoughts seem clumpy at times. If perfect syntax and spelling are your thing, then I apologize in advance. I am doing this book on a skeletal budget and a time crunch, and frankly, I can't afford perfection at the moment. I hate formatting on my own as well. I wish my editing skills were as good as my words sometimes.

Hell, the whole book is basically about how life isn't perfect, so a minor screw-up here and there should not condemn my words as irrelevant because of minor miscues. I promise you this. You stick with me in this book, and I will outline my case uniquely for wanting my money and the case for so many people impacted by the same type of issues with the system. I help these people daily, and now it's time to help myself in the only way I know how.

CONTACT INFO

James Baca

"The Notorious Banker" Podcast
Available on Spotify, Apple, Google

Twitter: @BankBetterGuy

Contributions to my Project:

Patreon: Patreon.com/NotoriousBanker
CashApp: $TheNotoriousBanker
Venmo: TheNotoriousBanker

The Notorious Banker
P.O. Box 14214
Las Cruces, NM 88013
e-Mail: thenotoriousbanker@gmail.com

A portion of the proceeds of this book will go to The Play Lab, where my late niece's "Ariya's Corner" which was dedicated earlier this year. I will also donate a portion of the proceeds to combat food insecurity in my home state of New Mexico through various organizations Follow my Twitter for more info on that.

HOW WE GOT HERE

Jefferson D'Arcy.

That was my default vision of an unemployed guy for years until I became one in 2018. Jefferson was a man who seemed to skirt by life with a smile and a few schemes with his neighbor Al Bundy on the TV Show, Married With Children. It wasn't a real unemployment experience. Although the actor Ted McGinley played the role well and should be applauded for all the character roles he had over the years, I can tell you, unemployment isn't easy, even if you have good looks like him and a banker wife like Marcy.

Unemployment sucks. Looking for a job sucks. Paying bills sucks. Trying to figure out what you want to do for the rest of your life sucks. I know all of this. A lot of you know all of this.

While my 1980s/1990s TV reference may be lost on many of you, I can assure you that life doesn't imitate art. Unemployment brings on insecurity and challenges to your physical and mental health if you don't care for yourself. Worst of all, there is this perception that you are some slovenly person watching the boob-tube, playing slot machine games on your phone, waiting for your mom to bring you some leftovers to eat.

It's been an interesting chapter in my life, but one that has made me better in so many ways. I have learned to be more "fiscally efficient" than ever before. A decade-plus in banking showed me the horrors of not watching your money and being forever in debt. A lot of my clients at Bank of America were beyond help. I lost five close customers to suicide in my time there, and all had financial issues. I think about every single one often. My mind gets upset. Why the FUCK should money matter so much?

It does, though. Such is life, and that's fine. But the

criticism I have seen of so many unemployed people since the pandemic began is frankly disgusting. Do people take advantage of specific programs? They do. But there is a story behind every person who seeks help. People should not rail against handouts without knowing the people asking for them. But yes, I have seen liberties taken in my lifetime.

My childhood in the early 1990s gives me memories of people holding steady jobs with the city of Socorro, NM (my hometown) selling food stamp coupons for cash, with a lot of them using the money to support drinking, drug, and gambling habits. It was customary to see these deals happen in front of the local grocery store. When food stamp benefits got attached to a debit card, it was commonplace to witness the handoff of a card from someone in another car to the person who bought the food for cash and waited for them to come out to get the card back.

I even have personal experience with someone taking liberties with a program, though in hindsight, I don't see much wrong with what she did now.

I love my mom to death. She worked hard to put food on the table after my parents divorced. We weren't homeless, but we had section 8 housing in the mid-1990s, and we lived in a crappy trailer on a hill, which was fifty feet from the train tracks. The weeds were as high as an elephant's eye to quote "Oklahoma," and if there was a rainstorm, we lived in a mud pit as our dirt driveway would be the envy of every 1990s strip club with every gallon of rainwater that fell. It sucked so bad. My mom tried to do something to put a roof over our heads, and while it was terrible, I am thankful for it today.

One of the caveats of public housing then (and I assume now) was that the housing was subject to inspection to make sure you met all the requirements to live there with your kids. You know, food in the house, electricity, water, and making sure it doesn't look like extended footage from "Hoarders" in there. Understandable. One of the things that were part of the inspection was to ensure no other people were living in the house, i.e., boyfriends/girlfriends/buddies. I didn't get it then, and I don't get it now.

My mom did have a boyfriend who was living in the trailer. He became my stepdad and father to my sister, Vanessa. He was a ranch hand six days a week, busting his ass to make minimum wage. He was a naturalized citizen of the US, and he would go on to stay with my mom for almost 13 years. He was a good guy to me and my brother, for the most part, helped put food on the table and better our living environment, and was decent enough to be around until the perils of drug abuse ultimately claimed his life a few years ago. I never had a flaw that I would point out about him, though my teenage angst would try to look for flaws.

Anyway, anytime these inspections, which in hindsight, are very invasive of one's privacy, were done by these liaisons who worked on behalf of the programs, it became a big thing at home. My mom understood that what she was doing was against the rules, and I guess, in turn, violated the program's rules and could theoretically get us kicked out. So, every pre-inspection night, my stepdad would hurry off to a friend's house, and my mom would go through the chore of relocating all of his clothes into my closet.

An insecure 12-year-old James was now the owner of a wardrobe of a short, overweight rural Mexican man. My mom filled my closet with cowboy hats that would make the Tejano music scene jealous and pointy "Cockroach Killer" boots, as my friends would call them that looked like the wrestler The Iron Sheik styled my stepdad.

I remember the damn look the inspector gave me when they opened my closet. The sports jerseys they likely expected were not in there. Instead, I had jeans stained with grass and horseshit. I had a vast collection of snakeskin clothing and nothing that said, "Hey, I'm in middle school!". It was a surreal experience and even weirder to think about it now.

Whether my mom did a good job hiding the fact that Mundo lived there, or maybe the inspector just not giving a shit, we will never know. She passed, and we got to live in that house rent-free for seven years while my mom toiled away as a french fry cook at a restaurant. In 2000, my mom got a home loan for a dream house for us kids with Countrywide Home Loans, which became part of my future company Bank of America (fodder for a forthcoming book) and caused her credit to implode when their subprime mortgage caused her to foreclose. I can't wait to tell that story.

Funny enough, the landlord of that trailer we lived in was the uncle of someone who became my best friend in high school, James C, who many called "Chavez." It was unique to see "the system" at work from all sides at that point because all these programs are here to help people. In all honesty, the people who helm the programs have to want to help others, even if the people needing help don't always follow all the rules.

Covid-19 blew up the way I thought of these programs because I have learned that it's not about who needs help but who gets lucky enough to get picked. Simple as that. A lot of my consumer advocacy work as The Notorious Banker online deals with how banks charge fees incorrectly on those who can't afford to pay hundreds a year to the bank. I also focus on people who have fraud claims with the bank that are ignored and denied through no fault of their own, simply based on time and desire for the bank to help that individual.

I saw it firsthand while working at Bank of America. My boss was always on my case for me volunteering to help my clients with service issues in the branch instead of pawning them off to a 1-800 number and an anonymous helper who doesn't know the subject entirely as I do. I would get a write-up for not hitting a daily (or hourly) sales goal, and part of the critique was that I was too busy helping "cloggers" with service issues and not sales. My regional manager referred to clients needing help as "cloggers," as in "clogging the toilet." I still get pissed to this day thinking of that phrase.

I was OK with getting verbal warnings if it meant I could impact the life of a couple of people every day. I would always make up my sales numbers and fund my bonus every quarter, but at the same time, I thought that these people trusted us with their money, so I am going to do what it takes to help them. I wasn't helping millionaires. A lot of my clients were homeless. There was a homeless shelter a couple of blocks from my branch. 999 West Amador is where a lot of my clients called "home" when they didn't have one, pass through every year looking for help.

What people don't get is most homeless folks likely have bank accounts, and various reasons keep them on the street. Many of them are vets or older folks, or people just forgotten by society, not given a break from the systems made to help people. It changed my outlook of someone sleeping on the ground forever, seeing the financial health of someone without a home. My area surrounding my branch also had a lot of low-income housing and halfway houses along the road to my old bank, which is now an art studio. Why is it an art studio?

Bank of America closed my branch in 2018 and continues to eliminate branches elsewhere. They have been citing a "migration to digital platforms" as a reason for the closure. I believe that is false. The majority of my clients were computer illiterate, or homeless, or preferred a physical branch. We knew our clients because, like me, a lot of us were there for years. Our numbers proved it to be false. It didn't matter, the branch on the "nice" side of the town remained open, we were promised transfers to other locations, and one by one, except for our branch manager, we were forced out of the company—a sad end to a fun career.

I was devastated when I got fired because I thought I would grow old there and always work hard for those who needed our help. Big businesses don't care about those things; it is more about making the most money without spending a lot. Simple as that. Tellerless branches exist in some markets as many people are feeling underbanked and unbanked in areas they never believed could happen. That's where a lot of my Notorious Banker work comes in online. I show people how to overcome these obstacles, and I do a damn good job at it.

Three days after I got fired, August 19, 2018, and one good cry on my wife's shoulders later, I decided to do two things that Monday: Donate plasma and apply for unemployment. I will talk about plasma in an upcoming chapter, but it's an underrated way to earn money when you don't have a lot of money. Unemployment, I believed, was a bridge too far for me at that moment. I have seen over 100 people in 13 years get fired by Bank of America that I worked with, and only one person got unemployment approved without a fight from BofA. Everyone else was up shit's creek, as I kept in touch with 90 percent of my coworkers from that time.

I was scared, but I decided to do it, as I entertained the notion of finding another bank to manage in this town. I made the call to the NM Department of Workforce Solutions (I will be shortening their name to NMDWS in the interest of brevity) that afternoon, my arm still bandaged from the plasma donation. By the way, side note, I hate the word "Solutions." Big banks use that phrase as a nom de plume for upselling clients, and I have a negative opinion of the phrase. Might I suggest a better name?

The menu on the phone was easy enough to navigate. I can't say that about most things these days, and I got placed on hold for the next available associate. Within 5 minutes, I was on the line with an accommodating woman. Her voice indicated someone middle-aged at the minimum, as the softness in her voice indicated a willingness to help. People must understand that when someone is calling for unemployment, that means some shit went down in someone's life, and you HAVE to be empathetic to their "life event" no matter if you know the whole story or not—basic customer service 101.

She took down my information and asked if I quit or if Bank of America fired me. No doubt in my mind, and anyone else's mind, I was fired. She asked why. The reason I was given was "Abuse of Override Privileges." My understanding was an incident that May where I got approved for override privileges to assist myself and others in opening accounts if something were to pop up under ChexSystems if the primary manager was away at lunch or on vacation. If a Social Security number flags on that system, my override would consist of asking a client for the physical card to match what was on the screen and verify it was input correct. I did it 100s of times for me and others.

Allegedly one day, I neglected to put a hyphen or "dash" on a driver's license input for a new client for the State of Indiana, which has them on license numbers. I overrode my account opening, and apparently, some back-office flagged my work as an abuse of power. Five days after getting wind of this accusation, BofA fired me. It was the dumbest way to lose a job because the computer system fills in the - for you when typing in a number from the state with an alphanumeric license number. So, it was a lie BofA told. (More in my future book)

If the branch had not closed and had there been more offices for bankers in the other branch, I would still be there today. I was the longest-tenured, highest-paid banker there, and

I had one fatal flaw here in Southern New Mexico. I was not fully bilingual. The two younger, cheaper bankers were.

(I understand and can speak Spanish somewhat. BofA has an INSANE Spanish language assessment you must pass to be certified to help Spanish-Speaking clients. I could never pass it.)

I said to the operator, "Branch closed; they decided to terminate redundancies in certain roles." There was no lie there. She understood. She mentioned she was from my hometown. The beautiful thing about New Mexicans is you feel a kinship with a stranger when they share your hometown. Call ended. My application was submitted for unemployment benefits. One day later, I got approved for 26 weeks at $433/week. $11,258 was coming to me to help bridge the gap between jobs. I was so thankful. I was also awaiting about $5,000 from BofA that was supposed to come to me for hitting my Q2 2018 sales goal and my unused vacation time.

I had postponed my vacation, which was to take place on August 9th, my wedding anniversary to be there when the branch I worked at closed down on August 7th, and I was to be there to move files and turn in keys and get keys for the other branch. Who knew that one week later, they'd push me out.

Bank of America has sent me no check for the money owed and never did to this day. I once received a paycheck from them for $11 in 2019 stating that they owed me for dozens of hours of backpay, but the check stub contained a ton of unintelligible "deductions" from that pay. Ironically enough, them paying me in 2019 ended up being a reason I got Pandemic Unemployment in Spring 2020

I wanted to pick my next job intelligently—one where I could make a difference. I wanted to make sure I worked for an ethical company, not a train-wreck like BofA, which railroads poor people and people of color daily.

I am good with money, and $11,258 could last me a year if need be because I have less than $900 in monthly expenses, and I was going to be donating plasma as well. I was okay financially taking my time. Then something happened a couple of months into my paid unemployment. I found my calling.

Logging into Twitter, mainly out of boredom, I decided not to search for sports news or hilarious videos. I searched "Wells Fargo," still fresh off the fake accounts scandal. I then searched for "Bank of America," which, of course, is full of many problems that I saw firsthand. I was stunned. The complaints on both banks were endless and disheartening.

I saw people posting photos of their bank statements with hundreds of dollars of overdraft fees. I saw people pleading with the banks' Twitter accounts to get in touch with them because there were problems with their home loan, and no one would answer their phone calls locally. I would see people talk about how they were hacked and money wiped out from their accounts, and how for 90 days, their bank had not decided to approve the fraud claim, nor provided temporary credit in the meantime, so they were broke and unable to pay bills.

I am reminded of a Simpsons episode where Selma, Marge's sister, is dating a man. She is a chain smoker, and her fiance introduces her to cigars, which she says are like "smoking 20 cigarettes at once". An outdated analogy, but I felt that the consumer complaints of those banks had that 20x ratio that Selma mentioned as it pertained to sadness.

It was like I was living a BofA nightmare all over again. People needing help, and no one giving a fuck. It was surreal, and still to this day, three years into my journey, it is still surreal. It was like witnessing a car crash and saying, "Do I help?" which I debated for a few days.

I decided to try to help. I started with basic stuff at first. One person tweeted at Bank of America, "I need two years' worth of statements for the IRS. How do I go about getting them?" Twelve hours later, BofA neglected to respond. I finally did. "You can print out up to 2 years by going to your statements & documents screen on your account page. Anything else you need can be ordered at the branch for $5 per month per account."

A simple question like that was too hard for a multi-billion-dollar company to answer. I made the person happy and likely made her journey to deal with the IRS a little less complicated. The following person asked a more complex question about ordering a debit card. It was along the lines of, "Hey @bankofamerica. I am leaving for Europe in 3 days, and you blocked my debit card. I will have no way to function on my trip without one. Your branch associate said 5-7 days for a new one. I can't wait. HELP!"

I saw @bofa_help responding that there is no way to expedite the card, and they apologize for the inconvenience. It pissed me off because that was wrong. You CAN get a card faster.

BofA has this weird program on its system called STACI, which I only remembered because it shared my best friend's name from the bank, which allowed bankers to order cards the next day for a client for a cost of $15. My 2nd branch manager taught me that, and I then taught future bosses how to use it. I was considered the expert on how to do that task. I reached out to the customer, and I told her the steps she needed to do, and I gave her instructions to tell the banker in BofA nerdspeak how to access it.

Two days later, she got her card and headed to Europe, thanking @bankscrewedus, which was my handle at the time. I changed someone's existence with their money while sitting on a couch eating a Butterfinger. It was cool. There is no stupid boss to yell at me or belittle me for not overselling that person a travel credit card that would be no use to her. I was feeling good about this little project. I then changed my name on Twitter to @bankbetterguy.

Resourceful James said to himself, "How can I monetize this?". I wanted all the fun with helping people bank better while providing real-talk commentary about how to get better service from these people that claim to be there for their clients. I decided I would explore what I could do. I always liked to tell stories and give perspective about things that maybe are not known by a lot of people. In New Mexico, not a lot of people are bank savvy. Maybe talking about banking is something I can do to make money.

I was inspired by someone I can call a social media friend, Tim Dressen, from the podcast, "Five Hundy by Midnight," which is a podcast that talks about all things Vegas. I decided to start a podcast about lousy banking, bank news interpreted for the ordinary person and unethical customer service stories. It sounded far-fetched, but I know damn well, NO ONE IS DOING THIS TYPE OF CONTENT!

I named it "Why Your Bank Sucks," which was inspired (I'm inspired everywhere) by a famous article on the blog Deadspin called "Why Your Team Sucks," which talks about your favorite football team's flaws before the NFL season starts. I thought if I could be active on social media and help people while having a platform as to why you should rethink your banking choices, I could make a decent living. People can all rally around the fact that big banks suck. I then renamed it "The Notorious Banker"

I launched my podcast in December 2018, with zero sponsors and a couple of bank-related human-interest stories that I dissected. I advertised the hell out of it on social media, and guess what? I got lucky. I was averaging a few thousand downloads on every podcast. It would be easy to bring that number to sponsors, along with the integrated sponsorship my host company provided. I was happy that this could work.

My BofA unemployment benefits expired in February 2019, and at that moment, I decided to hit the phone to look for advertisers for my podcast. My salesmanship landed me a couple of smaller banks that wanted to stick it to the man as well on my podcast. That started in May 2019. We discussed fees, treatment of Iranian customers at major banks, which that podcast got me commended by the Iranian American Foundation, and other controversial topics that no one else was talking about with the background I had.

With the Iranian podcast being so critically acclaimed, I achieved about 10,000 downloads an episode. I was making several hundred dollars a month through clicks and sponsorships that I sold. I also had the public contribute to my Patreon page, as well as Venmo and CashApp. People would donate because they saw the work I was doing helping others, and there were times I was compensated for getting people out of jams when they could afford to give back. I was a banking mercenary, blowing up customer service roadblocks along the way.

2019 was an excellent year for me because it allowed me to play up my strengths and use a platform to educate, inform and entertain others. My next step to help others was clear. I wanted to sell myself as an "ethical sales coach." I love everything about sales, except the lying. I firmly believe that if you put everything out there factually, you can be more successful. I used that way of thinking while dating, and I landed an amazing girlfriend who became my wife, so I know it works.

I thought if I could get into smaller banks, teach them how to focus on sales while at the same time not selling your clients a bill of goods, I would kick some major ass. I wanted to think others could mimic my great work, and frankly, it was the one thing I believed I was qualified to teach. I already made some inroads by talking to some banks about this approach at the beginning of 2020.

Then, let me utter the phrase that many of you have probably said in the last year. It's four words.

Then the pandemic happened.

Inroads that I made to be an "ethical sales trainer" for smaller banks were nonexistent. Stay-at-home orders and the elimination of sales goals in 2020 at most banks, big and small, ruined what I wanted to do before I even got the chance to do it. I was terrified of what the pandemic would bring because I heard a podcast that predicted over a million deaths from COVID-19. While the world was still scoffing at the possibility, I watched the news every day and knew this time it was a little different.

I grew up in a primarily Hispanic state with elders who refuse to go to the doctor for every possible ailment until it is too late. I lost two grandparents to cancer that went unchecked until it was stage 4. I have two other grandparents in their 80s who won't go to the Doctor unless something falls off. I was scared. I didn't want to lose family members. I thought COVID-19 could be devastating for my community and the world because so many around me were the same with their health.

Do you know why I was more scared? I had $2,100 left in my bank account, and jobs would be non-existent for a while. I thought I was going to hit $0 in my bank account and show my wife that I didn't win this time. The bank which fired me 18 months prior got the last laugh. It was humbling and sad to say depression sunk in.

I was a man with a small business dream. I was living it, watching it grow in so many ways until it didn't exist anymore because of COVID-19. What was I going to do? Then, of course, in the middle of everything that the first month, a bill passed that would give a lot of workers unemployment benefits with a $600 bonus weekly from the federal government. That meant almost $1000 a week for 13 weeks. $13,000. Wow.

The great thing, of course, was that it was available to gig workers and self-employed folks. I was both in some senses at the time of the stay-at-home orders. I knew it was going to be great IF I could get it. But in my mind, I knew that there was going to be a big IF. I knew from my time at Bank of America when the shit hits the fan, somehow, everyone will be chirping in the same direction. I knew thousands of New Mexicans would flood the unemployment phone number with calls to see if they qualified and to apply.

I knew the website would be bombarded as well, and that stuff would not be updated with all the rules and regs regarding PUA, Pandemic Unemployment Assistance. So I waited a couple of weeks, and then on my 37th birthday, I submitted my application for benefits online and got a cover sheet to fax my documents in. I tried calling over 100 times on the first day to get through to ask some critical questions, and I got the same message after hitting the prompts.

"All of our associates are currently helping other

customers. Please try your call again later."

Then it would hang up. Why the fuck would it not let you stay on hold? Dude, I got a speakerphone and a lot of patience. I can wait 8 hours if I have to. Why are you cutting me off to only have me try and try again to hear the same thing, which does nothing but pisses off a person? It was ridiculous.

I lost my cool once during that week after a trip to Wendy's to get food with my wife. I was upset about the process, and I broke down crying on the way home because my $2.17 order of 2 6-piece chicken nuggets was something I was trying to tell myself I couldn't afford, and it hit home.

Man, I can't even afford $2.17 for fucking nuggets without making it an episode of "Shark Tank." It was humbling. People from back home used to tell me that I wasn't humble, even though I grew up with less than they did, and I finally realized that reality. It wasn't good.

I couldn't take it. Suicide crossed my mind, if only for a brief second. Funny enough, the news stories about bodies in cold storage for weeks, if not months at a time before they could be buried, likely talked me out of any notion of doing something like that.

I know I could "get a real job" when things settle down, but in March 2020, we didn't have the answer to that question, which is why the tension was incredible.
I am not living on the street. I have a fantastic four-bedroom house that my wife and I share in a nice neighborhood with good neighbors. I am college educated, as is my wife, who has an MBA from NMSU and is a big deal working for the university.

But I kept thinking back to my Bank of America days during that time. I felt that if someone walked into my office to open an account and wanted to deposit the same amount that I had in my account at the time of opening, my boss would chew me out for ONLY bringing in $2,100 "new money."

"James, you KNOW they have retirement somewhere. You KNOW they have resources elsewhere. You KNOW they have a mortgage. How come you didn't ask them to refinance their house with us? I got to question your commitment to this company if you are going to bring 'low-hanging fruit' like that to us."

Yes, my boss called people with no money "low-hanging fruit."

It stressed me out, so I decided that I would take an educated guess as to what the state needed to approve me for unemployment. It seems easy enough, but I know that if I make a mistake and get denied, it would be on me, and they would blame me for not getting help and making a mistake, and that would be the end of that. The people who are able to make those decisions don't know how those words cut into you when they are said to you. I had to give shitty news to bank clients daily at my former job, so I know what I am talking about there.

So, I fill out the paperwork, and I submit it using a company called Efax online. I spent $3 to fax it to get it to the state. It was my hail mary to get money to save me for at least a year and allow me to grow my brand in other ways while we sit and wait at home.

I check on April 30th. I WAS APPROVED! I let out a primal scream and a fist pump that would put Tiger Woods to shame. It was exciting. Remember, this was the time EVERYONE was asking for help, and people were not laughing at others in financial duress as they are as I write this in the fall of 2021. It was a cathartic moment in my life, and I cried for an hour afterward after telling my wife the good news.

I will discuss more in a later chapter the volunteering work I had done helping others in need all across the country with big banks, their state's unemployment systems, PPP Loans, and many other things. Social justice was also on my mind with the George Floyd thing going on.

Inequality is everywhere in the banking industry, and I became a fierce, vocal advocate of it. State unemployment systems are run mainly by major banks, with my home state of New Mexico included. Issues that would come up in banks came up every hour of every day for me with The Notorious Banker.

People sought my opinion, and in some cases, my help getting heard. I did a lot for a lot of people. I feel like I am earning my soul back.

Of course, the fed money ran out in July 2020 when Congress and President Trump couldn't agree. The gravy train was over, and it was sad, but I understood why we hit a roadblock. It's election season. I did figure a future Federal Pandemic Unemployment Benefit would happen down the road, though. It just made sense that we would see an agreement on that.

It was around that time where certain states started relaxing specific COVID-19 mandates, and the vitriol between people on different sides of the aisle was getting worse. I would see people in my hometown who were gainfully employed talking shit about those who needed help and couldn't get any more assistance. It was hard to see half of the people in my life mocking how people were struggling, whether it would be because of actually having COVID-19 or impacted financially because of it. It was fucking horrible.

Most of those folks got their jobs through friends, family, or other unethical means as well, so to hear them run their mouths was too much at times. The constant social media hate plus that election lead-up and the months after putting me in a huge funk, so much so, I couldn't watch the news anymore. It was that bad.

I cut ties with many people, not necessarily because of their views, but because they wallowed in negativity, a common occurrence with people in social media these days. I wanted happiness, and I wanted to show my worth to the world. Money-wise, I was still okay, not missing any bills, but I knew it would come to a head without help eventually. Plasma donating, and coupon clipping can only bide you so much time.

Then an agreement was reached in December, which allowed the PUA program to be up and running again as of December 27, 2020, and it would last until September 4th, 2021. It would be a $300 weekly incentive on top of qualifying unemployment. I did the math in my head, and I knew how much would be available to me if I qualified again, which I saw no reason why I wouldn't since I did earlier in the year.

My life would change, and even if I didn't max it out, I'd have time to get my project going full-speed ahead and have jobs training bankers, helping people with complex bank issues, and have advertisers on my podcast again. I had since renamed it "The Notorious Banker." The pandemic assistance would keep me nice and buoyant until we got there where I needed to be. I fully intended on honoring the system by continuing to look for work in the meantime, just in case.

I had a great Christmas with my family because I knew 2021 would be a great year. I knew it couldn't be worse than 2020. I was excited to start fresh and work on The Notorious Banker, helping people fight for their money while charting the course to exciting new adventures. I decided to log into the NM Department of Workforce Solutions website on December 28th, one day after we got the green light that the federal program was on again. I figured I would apply the same way as before. Nope.

I was prompted to change my password on the site, and when I did and re-logged in, I was told that my account was locked, and I had to call. I had to FUCKING call. The simple fact I had not gotten through once the whole year meant that I knew this would be a battle to get what was rightfully mine.

Buddy, you have no idea what I've been through, so let me tell you.

MY 9-MONTH NEAR-FRUITLESS JOURNEY FOR HELP

To say that the customer service system is broken is a massive understatement. At my previous employer, I felt like Bank of America had 204,000 employees, of which about 203,500 of them did absolutely nothing to help people. They were there for sales and revenue growth. I made calls on behalf of clients from my office, putting them on speakerphone to see how my clients were being helped. I saw how people were routed repeatedly to wrong departments, placed on hold for hours at a time, only to be told incorrect information to get off the phone. I would then interrupt the conversation between client and customer, state my name and bank ID number, and ask the associate why they gave my client incorrect information.

I was different than most. I was accountable and worked hard to help my clients get answers. I was firm, I was a leader, and I got results. At Christmastime, I would get fresh baked cookies, gift cards to restaurants, and most importantly, sincere holiday cards from clients telling me how important I was to their success. It was a great feeling.

2020 made me feel that way again for the first time in a long time. Although not a lot of money was earned aside from the unemployment benefits, I would work about 16 hours a day to help people get help during the most challenging times ever to get help from the bank. Much of my work had to do with people who needed help bypassing these phone systems designed to make them hang up and reach out to people who can help more directly.

Bank of America and Wells Fargo claim that some departments had a ten-fold increase in jobs to handle the call volume. While I don't dispute that, I can say that cross-selling was also a big part of those calls, and service was deemphasized.

Clients were on hold in other instances, hours at a time, only to be picked up and hung up on in a matter of seconds.

A person I talked to at Bank of America told me this happened with some employees to lessen their ACT or average call time. It was a way of goosing the system to show your bosses that you were efficient with your calls, mainly to help balance out your numbers when a client kept you on the phone for a long time. It was disgusting when I heard it, and it made me reflective of all the times I would see or hear of this happen years ago.

The funny thing is that a lot of my work helping people with bank issues showed me the true work ethic of many call center employees. Now, don't get me wrong, some incredible people in my life started in call center environments, and some are still thriving in that field to this day. However, my hometown of Las Cruces, NM, and my previous job at the bank introduced me to many people who you would NEVER believe could deliver effective customer service in a million years. Simple as that.

I don't think it's elitist of me to call folks out like this because I was not the best at service for a long while. It's just you can tell in interpersonal interactions how someone would be to other people. For the longest time, it was a running joke at my branch. We would call Volt, a call center in the nearby Wells Fargo tower, "Electric Chair" because all the employees we knew from Volt looked like felons, and in some cases, were ex-cons. They fit central casting for ex-cons, with tattoos, gruff demeanor, and the like. Many of them were cool, but you would never peg these people for skilled technicians with Apple, which is what Volt was doing in their call center at that time.

If there was a shortage of "qualified" workers for call center roles in 2018, I could only imagine in 2020 that the apple tree was picked clean. I suppose with the insane volume of calls coupled with the lack of skilled workers available to answer those calls; it was a no-win situation for the Department of Workforce Solutions in New Mexico, which is what I was calling to get my unemployment.

According to an article in the Santa Fe New Mexican,

from March 2020 to March 2021, the department received 18 MILLION CALLS. (!!!) Out of those 18 MILLION CALLS, only 6.6 percent of them were answered. That means over 16,000,000 calls were left unanswered, and the unemployed applicants were left calling over and over again because the phone system hung up on them. Wow. It's fucking unbelievable.

This is from the article:

"It has been constantly hiring and training new employees since the beginning of the pandemic, raising the number of call center agents from 84 to 176, with more coming. It hired contractors and brought in volunteers from other state agencies to help resolve issues, and of course, McCamley himself has jumped in."

McCamley is Bill McCamley, a resident of my hometown of Las Cruces, who was the head of the NM Dept of Workforce Solutions. Shortly after that, he left the role, and Ricky Serna, another well-educated gentleman, took his place. As you can see, according to the paper, when the shit hit the fan, McCamley pulled a Notorious Banker and said, "Screw it, I am going to try to help some of these people myself." I respect him for that, and it laid the groundwork for writing this book because of my horrific journey to get help—more on why later.

The number of employees being only 176 folks and still having to field millions of calls seemed like a recipe for doom. How many folks were discouraged to stop calling hundreds of times? How many just said to themselves that it was impossible to get help, so why try anymore? I understood the arduous task the employees had on their plate, as most calls are not quick 30-second calls. Most of these calls require ID'ing the client and answering several questions they may have. Although the associate answering the call may seem repetitive, answering the same "stupid questions," it was likely that unemployed individuals only time to get helped one-to-one like that, so call center employees to have to respect their customer's time and answer.

So how do I feel about my journey through the toll-free number of NM Department of Workforce Solutions and the "help" I received? Well, not good. It was likely the most frustrating customer experience of my life, and I have been through nearly losing my house because of a bank error. I was in awe at the near impossibility of getting help from December 2020 to September 2021. There was a single bright spot, but the rest resembled the dark forest from "The Wizard of Oz."

So, as I mentioned in the last chapter, I assumed that when the federal PEUC/PUA $300 weekly benefit kicked in, I would likely not talk to an associate to get helped. I figured that much like Spring 2020, I would have to apply online and hope for the best. There would be no variation to my plan because, frankly, there was no variation to qualify for the program if you were a gig worker or self-employed.

With my online portal locked, I immediately grew upset because I knew what that meant. That meant that I would have to overcome Powerball-like odds to get on the phone and connect with an associate that could help me unlock my online login to unemployment and not even take my application at that point. So, it was an extra step to have to traverse before we got to the REAL step 1.

I won't bore you with a daily log of my efforts, but from December 28, 2020, until April 12, 2021, I called no less than 600 times to the phone number of the Department of Workforce Solutions, which is 1-877-664-6894. I have dialed that number so many times, it has become burned in my brain, and it is no manageable number to memorize. Shout out to the WCW Wrestling Hotline for having an easy number when I was a kid. 1-900-909-9900. My parents would get mad at me for running up the phone bill with that.

Every morning it was the same. I should say every morning that I was allowed to call. It was the same thing. Monday, Thursday, and Friday, it was waking up at 7:50 am, staying in bed with eyes half-open until 7:58 am, when I'd start dialing the number. It was funny that the portal "opened" at 8 am, but the lines were jammed two minutes before that. I would call 10-12 times before I got out of bed.

Feb 11	11:34 AM	877.664.6984	Las Cruces, NM	Toll-Free, CL	2	--
Feb 17	4:22 PM	877.664.6984	Las Cruces, NM	Toll-Free, CL	1	--
Feb 17	4:22 PM	877.664.6984	Las Cruces, NM	Toll-Free, CL	1	--
Feb 18	7:00 AM	877.664.6984	Las Cruces, NM	Toll-Free, CL	1	--
Feb 18	7:57 AM	877.664.6984	Las Cruces, NM	Toll-Free, CL	2	--
Feb 18	7:58 AM	877.664.6984	Las Cruces, NM	Toll-Free, CL	1	--
Feb 18	7:59 AM	877.664.6984	Las Cruces, NM	Toll-Free, CL	1	--
Feb 18	8:00 AM	877.664.6984	Las Cruces, NM	Toll-Free, CL	1	--
Feb 18	8:05 AM	877.664.6984	Las Cruces, NM	Toll-Free, CL	1	--
Feb 18	8:12 AM	877.664.6984	Las Cruces, NM	Toll-Free, CL	2	--
Feb 18	8:53 AM	877.664.6984	Las Cruces, NM	Toll-Free, CL	1	--
Feb 18	9:21 AM	877.664.6984	Las Cruces, NM	Toll-Free, CL	1	--
Feb 18	3:09 PM	877.664.6984	Las Cruces, NM	Toll-Free, CL	1	--
Feb 18	3:10 PM	877.664.6984	Las Cruces, NM	Toll-Free, CL	1	--

The prompts were 1, 1, and 3, then enter your social security number. I can do all of that in 1 minute 12 seconds. Then I would hear, "All of our representatives are currently assisting other customers, please try your call again later." and then I would be hung up on. Every hang-up was another knife deep into my heart, as I lost faith several times throughout the process.

First of all, the way that people had only certain days to call was stupid. My social security number ends in one of the first three numbers, so I was allocated Monday as my call day. I could also call Thursday or Friday as make-up days for those who couldn't get through during their assigned day. Who knows if there are more people unemployed with the first three digits than the rest of them? It is an inexact science that they are using to try to even out the calls throughout the week. For that reason, I paid for it. I couldn't get through.

PLEASE TRY YOUR CALL AGAIN LATER

STATE OF NEW MEXICO
NEW MEXICO DEPARTMENT OF
WORKFORCE SOLUTIONS
PO BOX 1928
Albuquerque, NM 87103
www.dws.state.nm.us

James Baca

Las Cruces, NM 88012

February 09, 2021

Claimant id: 2000127705

Monetary Determination

You have been determined eligible for Continued Assistance Act benefit extension for Pandemic Emergency Unemployment Compensation (PEUC), you are eligible in accordance with the PEUC program authorized by Section 2107 of the CARES Act of 2020, Public Law (Pub.L.) 116-136, signed by the President on March 27, 2020. The Continued Assistance Act added an additional 11-weeks of benefits available under the PEUC program from 13-weeks to a grand total of 24-weeks.

As of this time, the PEUC program expires on March 13, 2021. If you receive a PEUC payment for the week ending March 13, 2021 and have remaining weeks on your claim, you may be eligible to participate in a phaseout period and may continue to collect PEUC through week ending April 10, 2021 or until your balance reaches zero or you reach 24-weeks of PEUC, whichever comes first.

Benefit Year Effective Date:	8/19/2018
Benefit Year End Date:	8/17/2019
Weekly Benefit Amount:	$433.00
Maximum Benefit Amount available during your benefit year:	$4,763.00
Dependency Allowance:	$0.00
Monetary Appeal Period Ends:	Wednesday, February 24, 2021

(Letter dated Feb. 9, 2021 affirming my eligibility for extended benefits. I did not receive this until April in my online portal and was never able to certify benefits off this request.)

  I would try 10-15 times at lunch and 10-15 times before their closure at 4:30 pm, all to no avail. I would get so pissed off. I would try to help people with their bank issues with my Notorious Banker project, all while calling the number incessantly. I would be hard to talk to, as my wife can attest. It was this lingering feeling that I was being left behind when I deserved the money as much as the next person, and it got to me.

  My brain started thinking about conspiracy theories in April. Seriously, I thought, "Maybe if I call from someone else's phone, it will go through." It was not like me to whip up these far-flung theories, but two days after, I thought that, on April 12, 2021, I had my wife use her cell phone to call at the same time as me. Within a couple of tries, she got through the gauntlet, and I chuckled, thinking my conspiracy theory was an apt one.

  I couldn't believe that I heard real hold music. It was a miracle. I was ecstatic beyond belief. It took a little more than an hour, and about 11 am, someone finally picked up. Still unshowered and unshaven, I ran to the main bedroom and laid down on the bed while the operator answered.

"Thank you for calling the New Mexico Department of Workforce Solutions. My name is Stephanie. My ID number is 1223849. How can I help you today?"

Stephanie was going to be my ticket to happiness, and it only was going to take four months of suffering, or so I thought. I explained the situation about being unable to access the web portal because it had been locked. She mentioned it had been a common problem for a lot of people. I can understand that, and to have an associate acknowledge it is one way of making the person you are helping feel better about it. She asked me when the last time was I got benefits. I answered, and the call was breezing through a lot of rapid-fire questions.

When we got to the end, she told me that she unlocked it for me to certify for benefits within 24 hours. I was so pumped. She told me to log in to see if I could see a different screen before she hung up. I could indeed see the main screen. She exclaimed, "I'm so happy for you. Thank you for your patience with it." Before I hung up, I asked her if I would have to apply again to make sure I could certify. She said yes, and I decided now was the time to end the call. I knew that tomorrow would be the day I could get things done.

So, I wake up the following day, excited to run to my home office and log in and finally get all this shit done and not have to worry about a phone call again. I logged in, easy enough. I go to the screen to apply for unemployment. Fill out all the things the same way I did in March of 2020. Done. From my last time receiving benefits, I know that it usually takes a day to get approved, and then I could certify.

So, the day after that, I logged into the portal again, this time hoping to certify. I couldn't. The buttons were greyed out, so I couldn't click on them. You got to be fucking kidding me. It was the most upsetting day because it felt like it would drag on again, with no end in sight. I started justifying in my head what could be going on.

"Maybe they laid off some workers because claim numbers are down, and it takes longer than it normally would get approved again."

"Maybe they are working at approving my backpay from December to April before I am allowed to certify for this current week. Yeah, it makes sense."

I was trying to justify any possible reason it wasn't going my way in my head as a means of protecting myself from the intense stress I had during the last several months of trying to no avail. Being optimistic was the only thing I had at the moment because it seemed by the genuineness of Stephanie on the phone and her ease of answering my questions that it was only a matter of time. I would get my money eventually. I felt confident about that.

STATE OF NEW MEXICO
NEW MEXICO DEPARTMENT OF
WORKFORCE SOLUTIONS
PO BOX 1928
Albuquerque, NM 87103
www.dws.state.nm.us

James Baca
Las Cruces, NM 88012

April 16, 2021

Claimant id: 2000127705

Monetary Redetermination

You recently submitted an application for Pandemic Emergency Unemployment Compensation (PEUC1) Benefits.

Upon review of your application for Pandemic Emergency Unemployment Compensation (PEUC), it has been determined that you are monetarily eligible for 13 weeks of PEUC benefits in accordance with the PEUC program authorized by Section 2107 of the CARES Act of 2020, Public Law (Pub.L.) 116-136, signed by the President on March 27, 2020. The Continued Assistance Act increased the maximum amount of benefits available under the PEUC program from 13 times your average weekly benefit amount to 53 times your average weekly benefit amount.

As of this time, the PEUC program expires on September 4 , 2021. The Continued Assistance Act increased the maximum amount of benefits available under the PEUC program from 13 times your average weekly benefit amount to 53 times your average weekly benefit amount. If you receive a PEUC or PEUC-A payment for the week ending September 4 , 2021 and have remaining entitlement on your claim, you may be eligible to participate in a phaseout period and may continue to collect PEUC through week ending September 4 , 2021.

(Letter Dated April 16, 2021 once again affirming my eligibility. This letter did not show up until July 9th, when I FINALLY got through to customer service.)

My 38th birthday came and went on the 21st of April, and a week and a half after I finally hit the promised land of speaking with a real-life person, my spirits were in the dumps. It seemed like it was all a pipe dream at this juncture. However, two days later, on April 23rd, I went to get my mail from the community mailbox on our cul-de-sac. It was a letter from the midwest. Unmarked. All my years working at a bank told me this was a card. It HAD to be my unemployment debit card. I had asked for a direct deposit into my checking account, but honestly, I could care less. I HAD MY CARD!!!

  I follow the prompts to activate the card, which is golden with red chile ristras on the front. It is a Wells Fargo card and a card I am familiar with from my work. Once activated, I call the number on the back of the card, because as I told my wife, I bet that it is pre-loaded with the money they owed me in backpay. Follow all of the prompts to listen to my balance.

(In robotic voice)

"As of April 23rd, your current account balance is zero dollars and zero cents. If you would like to hear your balance again, press pound."

Zero dollars? Why fucking send the card? I don't get how I did something right to generate the card into being issued. I know it's all automated in some sense, but obviously, all of the tumblers clicked correct, and suddenly, a Wells Fargo debit card was in my name. It was bizarre beyond belief. This card doesn't happen unless something was green-lighted somewhere.

So the next day, I set up the card's online banking portal through EPPIcard's website. When I say this website looks outdated, your brain instantly has a PTSD flashback to a modem making screeching noises and hours to download one MP3. It was and still is horrid looking. You can only create a username with seven characters max! It's like that old joke where someone would say another person is so old; their social security number is 2. I set up my name and password and went to the main splash screen. My current account balance is... NEGATIVE 50 FUCKING CENTS!!!

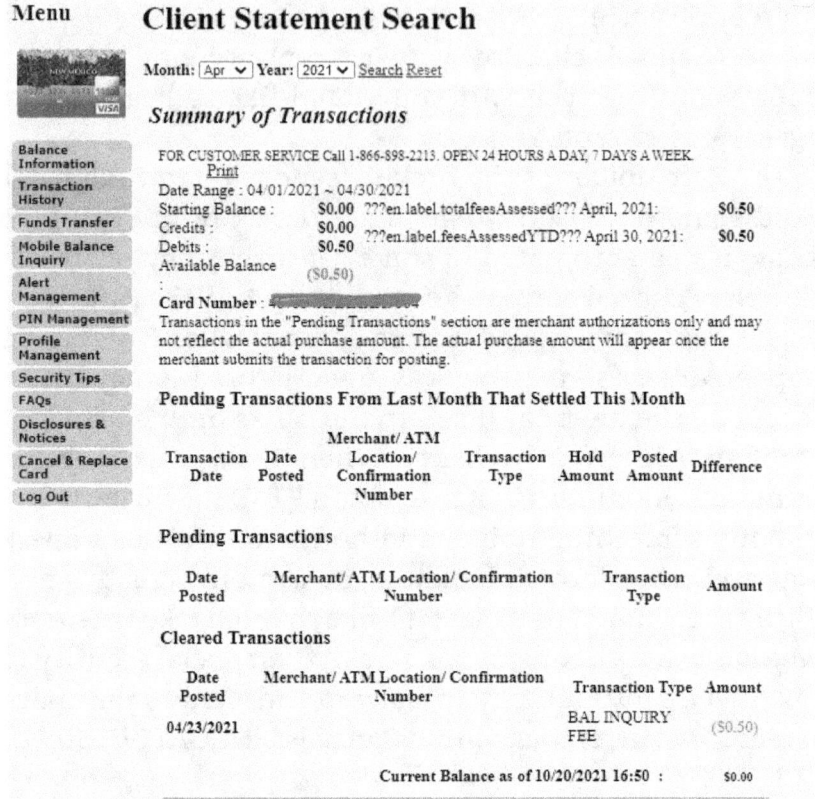

(Cool 1990s Era Website New Mexico has to check your card balance. This is for a card they issued despite their assertion they never approved me in Spring 2021. I owe 50 Cents.)

So, with most cash-pay cards, there are hidden fees for everything. It makes a consumer account at a big bank look like the sample tray at Sam's Club. You get a fee for checking your balance on the phone. You get a fee for using your card two times a day, and you get a fee for not using it at certain ATMs. Unbelievable. So now, not only am I not with my unemployment backpay, I am currently in arrears by two quarters to... Who? Wells Fargo? The state? Who do I owe for a call about a card I didn't think would come and I didn't know had anything in it?

Just for all the little fires that burned from this shit show, I was mad. I was angry. It's unacceptable to treat someone in need like this. As I mentioned, my experience in banking had prepared me with low expectations for customer service everywhere. Still, how the New Mexico Department of Workforce Solutions continuously failed me cracked my tough exterior. I also know that I cannot be the only one going through this, but I am the only one dedicated to not letting this go.

I continue into all of May and June trying to call 1-877-664-6984 to see where my money is, why I still can't certify online, and if I owe fifty cents for getting duped with a debit card with no linkage to any unemployment money.

Finally, on Friday, July 9th, I am sitting in my super-hot office, not working to help anyone. I am depressed. I feel defeated that I literally went a year and over 1000 calls and still have not thoroughly helped. I think this money will never get in my hands, even though the feds say I am entitled to it. I have tears in my eyes, but not because of this situation. I am five weeks removed from losing one of the younger family members I had. I will explain further in an upcoming chapter. Life isn't fair. But I am not licked yet.

I dial the number for the 1,092nd time since December 28th, 2020, and it finally puts me on hold for an agent! It was the first time using my phone since 2018 and the first call since April where I thought all the bugs were fixed but ended up creating more.

After 2 minutes of hold music, an older man answers the phone. His name is Barry, and he sounds relaxed and calm as he introduces himself and asks me to ID myself. I have a good feeling about this call for a couple of reasons. I just felt that a person who is calm on the phone is not going to get flustered and make mistakes by extension. The second reason is kind of silly, but I will share it anyway. Barry sounded like a very nerdy, intelligent older white guy.

As a Mexican-American 30-something know-it-all, I have spent the better part of 25 years getting chastised by my "friends" for being smart, being a nerd, answering all the questions on "Jeopardy." What happens with bullies doing that to you is that you eventually have to dumb down your conversations to fit in and become a phony. The positive about

Barry answering the phone was that I could speak like I have a 150 IQ, and I can use $10 words that will get me respect as an intellectual equal. Chris Rock did a great bit about how educated people of color are treated by their contemporaries if they come from a tough upbringing.

"So fucking what if you are smart? Think you're better than me? You're just a little bitch!"

Yep, I heard these things growing up.

Scoff all you want at the last two paragraphs, but it is so true. I got to be nerdy, and it worked to my advantage. I spelt out all the shit I went through the last seven months, trying to stay even-keeled as Barry is. He used "empathetic language," a trait I was taught in banking training to deal with an upset client. He was going by the book to listen, offer suggestions, and own the conversation. That's what an authentic customer service experience should be. No, the customer is not always right, but you must treat every conversation with the same amount of respect.

He helped me slowly and methodically apply for unemployment benefits with PUA again. Took his time asking me questions and got me to the point where he asked if I wanted to backdate it. I, of course, said yes, as I had been trying to get these benefits for 27 weeks before this. We filled that part out. He asked, "What was the reason that you couldn't file for benefits before this request?" I answered simply with the truth.

"I was unable to reach an associate by phone and was unable to apply for benefits online because of a freeze on my login. I also didn't know how to figure out how to unlock it until I called."

This reason I gave would prove to be the thing that spurred me to write this whole damn book. I ended the conversation by asking the obvious question of when I should know that I was approved, and he was overestimating the timeframe. (I could tell in his voice),

"Probably ten days or so. Give or Take."

I was happy with it, so I let him go, and I felt like a weight had been lifted off my chest. I knew things would at least get moving at that point.

The next day, I logged in, and there was a certify button!!!! HELL YEAH!!! I checked the benefit total, and it mentions that I would be getting a $660/week total with the federal benefit with a total amount of $13,000 approved by the state, not including the $300. I was then able to figure out the amount of backpay I should be getting. It was $20,291. There was some paperwork I would have to submit to get that done, but I got the first certification of money in a long time.

STATE OF NEW MEXICO
NEW MEXICO DEPARTMENT OF
WORKFORCE SOLUTIONS
PO BOX 1928
Albuquerque, NM 87103
www.dws.state.nm.us

James Baca
LAS CRUCES, NM 88012-6281

July 12, 2021

Claimant id: 2000127705

Monetary Determination

You recently submitted an application for Standard Unemployment Benefits, however; because your weekly benefit amount is twenty-five dollars or greater on your previous Pandemic Emergency Unemployment Compensation Program (PEUC) claim you will continue to collect benefits on the PEUC claim.

(Approval in July. I was finally allowed to certify after months of being unable to. Wording is different that previous emails, however, which implies rep coded my unemployment as "non-pandemic" when applying, which made no sense to me.)

The money gets approved and goes into that stupid Chile Ristra debit card the next day. So...If the card was an error, why the fuck did the money know where to go so quickly? I neglected to mention my bank information was already on their site, so a direct deposit to my account should have happened—no big deal. I am just happy I have money going in. $660....I mean, $659.50. Goddamn balance inquiry fee. At least I don't have that go against my credit or something. I guess I should also note, there's a $5 fee for them to wire it from your card to your checking account, so Wells Fargo took $5.50 out of my money for mistakes not made by me. Great.

There was now the matter of submitting documents to get my backpay. I was given a cover sheet with my Application ID and my info. It mentions where to fax all these documents and suggestions of what I should submit. The fax is to be no less than two pages. I figured I had a decent story to tell, which of course, was factually accurate, and with documented problems with calling NMDWS by major newspapers, I knew that the narrative I had was going to be just fine.

I made it a habit that when someone, whether at work or school, asked us to do an assignment with a minimum number of pages/words, and I would fucking blow right past that. It was a nod to how comfy I feel writing and telling a story, coupled with the fact that I want to outshine everyone like always. It's human nature, you know. I decided I would make it at least 20 pages worth of content. I wanted to give them so much to look at that they said, "Fuck it, I'm not reading all of this. Approved."

It was a nearly foolproof strategy, save for a few holier than thou teachers in school who somehow saw it as an insult to them. I started prepping my documents that evening. There was to be no skimping on what I gave them. I gave them the following:

- Phone records detailing the 1000+ times I tried calling them to no avail. These were documented on my Verizon bill as 1-minute phone calls.

- A letter explaining the journey I had been on from the login being locked in late December to the unlocking of the account in April, sending a debit card with no approval, and my last interaction with them in July.

- A detailed list of all the places I looked for employment. Documenting where you applied or looked for work was waived until sometime in May 2021, but I still gave them everything from December until July.

- An itemized total of what I feel I am owed because of all these hurdles totaled $20,291.00 and included a breakdown of what I believed was due to me.

There was no doubt I felt confident that I would kill it with the relevant information. I believed that most people do the bare minimum to get through this part, but frankly, I ate and slept this issue because it had weighed on me for so long. I put it all together in a nice, tight PDF format and submitted it. Now we wait.

And wait. And Wait. And Wait. And Wait. And Wait. And Wait. And Wait. And Wait.

There is one "wait" for every week I waited until I decided to write this. 9 weeks. I wasn't given a firm timetable, but every clue in my body tells me that my stuff is NOT being looked at, and although I don't want to go "K" word on these people (Rhymes with Darren), I may have to save my money from going away.

After waiting for 4 of those weeks, I decided to try the 1-877 number again. Surprisingly, I got through on the first try. I get an answer from someone right away. I didn't get her name because she didn't offer it to me. (Probably against protocol) I asked bluntly, "I submitted my accompanying documents a month ago for my back pay, and I haven't gotten a decision yet. When can I expect it?"

I wasn't curt, because as I mention to my followers on social media all the time, the person you FINALLY get isn't the person who did something to you. Try to win them over and not alienate them right away.

She started identifying me before she could give me anything. We get to my address, where I live on a street with the word Gunsight in it. She says something straight-up bizarre.

"Is that a REAL address? It sounds fake!"

How the fuck do you even answer that? Of course, it is accurate, and if her computer is like any other major entity's computer system, it likely has the USPS database to cross-check if an address exists. I answer yes.

"Ok. I was just kind of skeptical."

This doesn't feel like it's going well. She is not doing basic customer service things you'd expect. I just want an answer. I just want to know if I am a sucker for waiting this long.

"So, Mr. Back-uh (Always mispronounce Baca), I can tell you that your request is processing and should be arriving at a decision in 4-6 weeks."

At this point, we are four weeks in, so I know the end should be here really soon. I thanked her for her time and hung up. It just never seems to have even one thing go remotely smoothly. It's August, and I am in week 4 of getting by $660/week current benefits while waiting for the back pay. I am adding to my bank account and mapping out bills that need to be paid with this money.

We come up to the end of the benefits on Labor Day weekend. I am sure that is no coincidence, right? I have put in nearly $4,000 into my account, which I am thankful for, but I am still missing a HUGE chunk of it, with no word from the state or no direct deposit alert to my phone. When I see my bank account start to whittle down, I get a little scared. I am not going to lie to you and say that I will be broke tomorrow without this, but I will be eventually.

I came up with a final decision on what I should do. I need to make moves to make sure I get in a request in time for them to look over my documents. I was aware that despite September 4th being the "last day" for people to apply, there would be a grace period for people to put in requests for their back pay still.

PLEASE TRY YOUR CALL AGAIN LATER

STATE OF NEW MEXICO
NEW MEXICO DEPARTMENT OF
WORKFORCE SOLUTIONS
PO BOX 1928
Albuquerque, NM 87103
www.dws.state.nm.us

James Baca
LAS CRUCES, NM 88012-6281

September 17, 2021

All COVID-19 related federal unemployment programs are **set to expire on September 4, 2021**. If you are currently receiving regular state unemployment you may continue to receive benefits under that program, depending on eligibility requirements. Federal programs ending regardless of account balance are the following:

o **Federal Pandemic Unemployment Compensation (FPUC)**: The week ending September 4 is the last week of unemployment for which the additional $300 weekly payment for any claimant that is eligible for at least $1 of an underlying unemployment compensation program.

o **Pandemic Unemployment Assistance (PUA)**: The week ending September 4 is the last payable week for PUA benefits which provides benefits for claimants who are not otherwise eligible for unemployment insurance, such as self-employed, contract workers and gig economy workers. For 30 days after this expiration, the Department will continue to take new applications so long as the period of unemployment benefits requested is before September 4.

o **Pandemic Emergency Unemployment Compensation (PEUC) and PEUC-A**: The week ending September 4 is the last payable week for PEUC or PEUC-A which provides an extension of benefits after regular unemployment compensation benefits have been exhausted. For claimants currently on regular state UI benefits, they will not be eligible for this extension for weeks of full or partial unemployment ending after September 4.

(Awesome letter on September 17th telling me to "be ready" for benefits that expired 2 weeks ago on September 4th. Letters like this confuse people into what is going on with their benefits.)

According to a story on KRQE, a local CBS affiliate in Albuquerque, there was still work on the pandemic pay at NMDWS. This was crucial to me as I hadn't heard anything still. I decided to write a letter to Ricky Serna, the head of the NMDWS, and who replaced Mr. McCamley earlier in the year.

I think 99% of my work as The Notorious Banker, a consumer advocate for bank customers, is about teaching people how to write effective letters to get attention paid to them. I knew that if I could be honest and genuine, and as long as the person on the other end even gives the tiniest shit about me, I would be fine. I used to tell people not to be afraid to ask because no is not the worst thing. Not trying is the worst thing.

This is what I wrote on September 28th, 2021, to Ricky Serna:

Claimant ID: 2000127705
Good afternoon,

My name is James Baca, and I am writing this almost as a last resort because I have waited for over 11 weeks for something to take four weeks. I applied for and received UI Benefits, with the $300 Federal Boost on July 9th until the end of the benefits on 9-4-2021. I, of course, since I was in the PEUC-A program, could not certify beyond that.

An associate over the phone helped me put in a request for backdated pay from December 2020 until the week before I finally got through to an associate. My online portal was locked, which I explained, and I could not complete the application sooner. It took no less than 1000 phone calls to the toll-free number to FINALLY get through (I submitted my phone records along with a manual log of my job search from that time frame even though it wasn't a requirement until May). I wasn't given a time frame on the status of the request.

I gave it a month, and in early August, I called back, and after over 100 attempts, I FINALLY got a different person. I was told it would be a 4-6 week process. I accepted that, as I am sure everyone in your department is quite busy. We are now in week five past that timeframe.

I can respect how much everyone has worked to get things done. I worked for a major bank, and a typical customer service day can be busy, so I can only imagine how a COVID-19-Amplified glut of people needing help can tax even the best customer service rep. I feel like something isn't right with the process, and I feel like something isn't getting done promptly.

I was torn as even to write this letter because I am sure you are busy yourself. It is a bit unorthodox for someone to write this to you seeking help (or maybe not... people are quite resourceful these days in finding contact information). Still, per the CARES act, I just purchased healthcare for the final 3 months of 2021 (the first time I have had full healthcare in 20 years since I was a minor). Frankly, the backdated money will go to taking care of some medical things plus paying the bills I have been unable to entirely since last March... Plus, if there is any left over, continue to either locate work or start a small business with my skillset to help others.

I don't want to ask for "special attention," I want to know the wheels are turning, and I can figure out how the rest of my year will *go, and by extension, the next chapter of my life.*

Thank you for your time. My information is below

Every single thing in there is true. The healthcare thing I will talk more about in an upcoming chapter. But I was heartfelt and respectful, taking him from his busy schedule to have him even read it. I just wanted a helping hand.

Part of what I do with Notorious Banker is I deal with people who are at risk of losing their home, and like clockwork, when a customer emails the bank in peril like that, they are always ghosted by the people who are assigned to help them. A lot of my work allows people to mount an offensive which includes emailing the rogue associate's boss, and if there is an extreme element to the story, I help them alert the media. I have gotten dozens of stories onto local TV across the country of bad banks doing bad things to bad people. It takes a certain kind of savviness to do what I do effectively.

There are so many cold-hearted bankers out there who can't even carry on a simple email reply about what is happening to someone needing help. I know the feeling of being ignored and helpless. I have lived it myself, through my clients while in banking, and now with my social media followers. I know when I am, or someone else is getting shafted.

Even if I am unsuccessful in getting help, it is not for lack of trying. I make sure I go down kicking and screaming. This writing exercise I am doing here is my kicking and screaming, helping point out the fatal flaws in our nation's unemployment systems, even beyond the pandemic.

The interesting thing here is that I know he read my letter because, within 16 hours of my email being sent, I got an automated email from NMDWS stating that there were documents for me to view in my portal. When I received the email, I had a massive needle in my arm as I was donating plasma for $60 at that moment. My phone wasn't opening PDFs, so I had to download a special browser to read what it said:

Notice of Determination Reasoning and Findings

After consideration of the facts submitted, it has been determined that your reason for not contacting this office to file your claim earlier does not constitute a good cause. Therefore, your request to backdate your claim has been denied. Your current date of claim is effective 08/19//2018, and you recently re-opened your claim on 07/04/2021. You requested a backdate effective to 12/28/2020. The reason for the backdate request is because you were unable to contact NMDWS or figure it out on your own. Good cause to backdate the claim has not been established and is therefore denied.

Applicable Section of Law Subsection A (1) of NMSA 1978 51-1-5 and NMAC 11.3.300.30

A waiting period may not be served nor benefits paid on this claim for any week before 7/4/2021.

You have 5 other outstanding issue(s) that may affect your eligibility for benefits.

Issue ID:0006 4230 30-01, Discharged - Lack Of Work

Issue ID:0006 4227 19-01, Reporting Requirements - BackDate Request

Issue ID:0006 4230 43-01, Still Employed - Self Employment

Issue ID:0009 2450 25-01, Discharged - Lack Of Work

Issue ID:0009 2450 40-01, Still Employed - Self Employment

Log in to your account at www.jobs.state.nm.us to check the status of the other issue(s). If you have any questions, please contact a Customer Service Agent in the Unemployment Insurance Operations Center at 1-877-664-6984, Monday through Friday, from 8:00 a.m. to 4:30 p.m. You can also access claims information online by logging in to your Unemployment Insurance Tax and Claims System account at www.jobs.state.nm.us. Please have your Issue or Claimant identification number available when you call.

So basically, I got fucked over. Nothing changed. Nothing. The further away we got from the time I tried to apply for benefits, it only cemented my case of being unable to get back on my feet for work. It is unconscionable. If I got approved for benefits on 7-9-2021, that means I was going through the same things before that day, and there was probable cause to approve me regardless.

STATE OF NEW MEXICO
NEW MEXICO DEPARTMENT OF
WORKFORCE SOLUTIONS
PO BOX 1928
Albuquerque, NM 87103
www.dws.state.nm.us

James Baca
LAS CRUCES, NM 88012-6281

September 30, 2021

Claimant Name: James Baca

Claimant Id: 2000127705

Issue Identification Number: 0011 3326 10-01

Employer: N/A

Appeal Due Date: October 15, 2021

Appeal Rights/Derechos De Apelacion. This determination is final unless appealed by the appeal due date above. You may file a request for a hearing by mail using a signed letter, completing the Request for Hearing information provided with this document, or by logging into your on-line account. Have your Issue Number when you appeal.

Notice of Determination

Reasoning and Findings

After consideration of the facts submitted, it has been determined that your reason for not contacting this office to file your claim earlier does not constitute good cause. Therefore, your request to backdate your claim has been denied. Your current date of claim is effective 08/19//2018, and you recently re-opened your claim on 07/04/2021. You requested a backdate effective to 12/28/2020. The reason for the backdate request is because you were unable to contact NMDWS or figure it out on your own. Good cause to backdate the claim has not been established and is therefore denied.

A waiting period may not be served nor benefits paid on this claim for any week prior to 7/4/2021.

You have 5 other outstanding issue(s) that may affect your eligibility for benefits.
Issue ID:0006 4230 30-01,   Discharged - Lack Of Work
Issue ID:0006 4227 19-01,   Reporting Requirements - BackDate Request
Issue ID:0006 4230 43-01,   Still Employed - Self Employment
Issue ID:0009 2450 25-01,   Discharged - Lack Of Work
Issue ID:0009 2450 40-01,   Still Employed - Self Employment

Log in to your account at www.jobs.state.nm.us to check the status of the other issue(s).

If you have any questions, please contact a Customer Service Agent in the Unemployment Insurance Operations Center at 1-877-664-6984, Monday through Friday from 8:00 a.m. to 4:30 p.m. You can also access claims information online by logging in to your Unemployment Insurance Tax and Claims System account at www.jobs.state.nm.us. Please have your Issue or Claimant Identification number available when you call.

HOW TO APPEAL THIS DETERMINATION

This determination is final unless an appeal is filed WITHIN FIFTEEN CALENDAR DAYS from the date of mailing of this determination. If the fifteenth day falls on a weekend or holiday, your appeal deadline will be extended until the next business day. Late requests for an appeal hearing will only be granted if it is established that there was good cause for the delayed request.

You may appeal by: logging into your online account at www.dws.state.nm.us, writing a letter of appeal and faxing it to (505) 841-8636 or by mailing it to: NMDWS Appeals Tribunal, P.O. Box 1928, Albuquerque, NM 87103. When submitting your letter of appeal, please include your name, mailing address, telephone number and identification number ("Claimant ID" for claimants or "EAN" for employers) as well as a copy of this determination. Be sure to sign and date your letter of appeal.

If you request an appeal on this determination and are a claimant, you must continue to complete your weekly benefit claims certification if you remain unemployed in order to protect your rights to benefits. If your former employer appeals a determination allowing benefits to you and the appeal decision is against you, you will be required to repay those benefits.

    The first idiotic part is the claim referring to my firing date from Bank of America three years ago. So much has happened since then. I don't get how they use that date as proof of what is happening with me or not happening.

    Then I had two seemingly contradictory "issues." Lack of work and still working, "Self-Employed." Which one is it? I can tell you no one currently employs me, and what income I gathered pre-pandemic showed my ability to earn money as a self-employed podcast host with my sponsorship money.

    However, the money dried up when the pandemic hit, so my money-making venture was taken away from me, and I had no sponsors since COVID-19 hit. I am doing my podcast for free. I am doing my consumer advocacy pro-bono, helping so many people with bullshit like this daily. I will receive $20 here and there from people grateful for the help, but that constitutes a gift, not a charge, and indeed not a business.

My work isn't under a business umbrella yet, though I was going to look long and hard about incorporating The Notorious Banker if and when I got my money from the state. You make lemonade out of lemons, and I intend on doing such a thing.

Something is royally fucked up with my application, and I have the footing to say I didn't fill it out. Barry, the nerdy phone representative, is the one who typed it up and submitted it. So basically, I am being held accountable for them not understanding Barry's wording of my situation.

And FINALLY…. The reason I backdated the request from last December was the simple fact that I could not get NMDWS on the phone. I tried over 1000 times to call. 1000! I have phone records showing these 1-minute calls, which hang up on you when busy beyond capacity. What this letter says is something one of my high school friends would say.

"Sounds like a YOU problem, James."

I chose consumer advocacy because someone will get this letter who doesn't know how to fight. Someone who doesn't know that something is seriously wrong with their decision-making process, denying you for bad information input on the application, and something that you can't control in the phone lines being off the wall busy because of the insane unemployment numbers. You are blamed for being in the wrong place, wrong time, and not graded for preparation.

I am writing this out, and it gets me more upset because I never feel like the victim in these cases usually. I fight back, especially when I know I am right. Someone in the state of New Mexico decided a legit excuse that NMDWS caused was my problem, and for that, I should not be eligible for the money I have been waiting on.

The debit card was sent to me. How do you explain that? I can hear an associate now. "We are sorry about the confusion. You weren't supposed to get that card." Ok, I'll believe you if you tell me what prompted the system to send that card involuntarily. The state won't be able to answer that. I saw enough horror stories on social media of people being forced to pay back their unemployment due to errors, whether from applicants or the state.

How can you be someone who must tell someone already desperate for money that it wasn't theirs, to begin with, and if you don't pay us, we are going to put a lien on your property and subject you to civil penalties? It's bank-like. It's cold. It's unforgiving.

I know damn well that the head of NMDWS, Ricky Serna read my email because how much of a coincidence would it be that after nine months of fighting for help, an email to the head honcho prompted someone to look at my file within 24 hours, and deny me? There was no phone call. There was no email reply. It's a PDF on a website with very little explanation of how they came to that conclusion. It did come with a notice that I can appeal, and I have to do so within 15 CALENDAR DAYS. We are on day 6 of that appeal timeframe as I write this. I intend on doing so, and I plan on finishing this book by then as well.

There is an inconsistency of service going on here. How can you be the head of a department when you don't want to get your hands dirty? In an interview, Bill McCamley, the head of NMDWS, reviewed applicants' records to help his team. That's a leader. Where is the leadership now?

I want my money. I want REAL HELP!

HOW CUSTOMER SERVICE HAS CHANGED SINCE COVID-19

I admit it. I was an excuse maker in my younger years. When I didn't want to go to school, I would blame it on feeling sick. I would blame it on bullies (although that excuse was more than valid). I would blame it on my parents' divorce. Yes, I sunk that low.

What's funny is that even at ten years old, I knew my parents getting divorced was likely the right move. I had an adult way of looking at things early on. I had conversations about finances with my mom before middle school. I knew even at that age I was born to listen and help people, especially with their money and life choices, because it was always easy for people to talk to me. For some reason, I have spent 38.5 years trying to figure it out.

When I graduated high school, I didn't immediately go to work or college. I wanted to take a break because "I hadn't in 13 years. I need to recharge." I didn't want to move out of town for school because "My parents and grandparents need me here to help them out." I didn't accept the first entry-level jobs because I wanted time for myself. To do what? I don't know. But these are things I used to do and kids always do.

If you can believe it, my apathy, brattiness, and laziness from elementary school until my early 20s were why I became good at customer service later in life. Why? Because I know that I didn't even give 100% of what I could've given my first few years at BofA, and I was still moving up the ranks fast. It was amazing. I was a success story for all of you slackers out there because I realized that you can still be kind of lazy and find success, and I did just that.

When I transferred to another location out of my

hometown, I knew that I had to turn it up a notch because at 25, if I fail, mom isn't going to be there with a grilled cheese that she stole from work for my sister and me. My grandma will not give me a handshake lined with a $20 bill anymore. She gave me that handshake until my mid-30s despite my success at the bank. Why did I keep getting it? Because it's disrespectful not to honor your grandma's wishes. Customer service would have to be my everything because there was no more safety net if I didn't do good enough.

I learned at Bank of America that the higher up you go, it almost seems like those people know what they can get away with without any repercussions. What do I mean? Branch managers discriminated against Black People who wanted to cash their paycheck, despite the man's other coworkers being able to before him. That was a viral Youtube video in 2019-2020, and through my Notorious Banker project, I found out that the manager who did that is still employed.

Why? Because the manager knew that person wasn't a "real" customer (one with accounts), so he could impose his rule how he wanted. There was no possible way this issue could escalate within the Bank of America complaint system because that non-client cashing a check isn't considered a customer by upper management. He skated on that.

It's the constant dick-waving I saw with fellow managers at Bank of America that made me despise that place. I saw people obsessive over sales, not the little old lady on partial social security fixed income asking for a $35 overdraft fee to be refunded. My branch was in an area with many people with no money, and I had to move mountains to refund anything at times because it was the right thing to do.

Customer service means that much to me. I don't go above and beyond to help people to be popular. I did it to show people that hard work pays off. Being kind can change someone's day, year, or life, and understanding that every person has different needs and you have to adapt your service at times.

The Los Angeles BofA racial incident only emboldened

my consumer advocacy work. The Notorious Banker thrives because there are stories like this every day in the world, not just in banking, that can be averted with just a bit of care and a little more consistent service.

Before my consumer advocacy project, I, too, was the person who bitched out companies for bad experiences on Twitter. Complaints can be an great and needed, but they can also be annoying without context. Not everyone is out to get you, but as I mentioned about my lazy/apathetic/slacker days, it only takes a little bit of effort to make something right.

What I do to help people with bank issues is take down information to develop a game plan. I ask what was said, cross-reference it with basic customer service routines and my bank training as a teller and manager, and I walk through the complainant what went wrong and how they should address this issue with their bank. I am the only person on social media who does this type of advocacy, and it's needed.

My slacker past and my experience with poorly managed banks allow me to identify when a customer is poorly treated systemically by the company, in an isolated incident by an individual or single location, or if it is all a misunderstanding. I've seen all sides of thousands of incidents since I started in 2018 and have been a party to 13 years of high-level customer support conversations before that.

All my ranting leads to this point: We have used the last year and a half to applaud people for outstanding work during COVID-19, and at the same time taken our hands off the wheel and caused our car to veer into a ditch because of piss poor service, accountability, and ownership.

The former NMDWS head, Bill McCamley, said in an interview that before leaving, he reviewed unemployment cases and interacted with people in need. My interaction or lack thereof with Ricky Serna, who helms it now, who didn't even bother to email me back, constitutes a SERIOUS issue in problem handling, ownership, and accountability.

This is in an environment where the number of people

filing unemployment claims has to be down at least 80%, which means fewer people, which means seemingly more time to help individuals and ask questions to get better help. No top guy should be afraid to get their hands dirty to help.

When I publish this book and call out the state, Serna, and NMDWS for not helping me properly, blaming me for things out of my control, and ignoring my pleas for help, I am sure the NMDWS will release a statement that looks like this.

(This is a parody)

The New Mexico Department of Workforce Solutions has gone above and beyond to assist hundreds of thousands of New Mexicans during these unprecedented times. We continue to provide a full staff to meet the needs of our constituents. However, because of limitations placed on us by time and by COVID-19 protocols, we cannot dedicate additional resources to a single individual's complaint beyond what is promised in our mission statement. While we cannot comment on an individual's specific case, the application and appeals process treat all constituents equally and fairly.

I just pulled that imaginary press release out of my ass, but I bet anything that gets said by the state will sound like that. You got to remember that I speak in PR Bullshit because I worked for a major bank. I know how to puff out my chest, address one person's concerns without ever really doing so, and say nothing of substance.This is how I was trained at BofA, and this is what I read EVERY DAY a bank messes up with my project.

Using COVID-19 as the excuse for not helping when COVID-19 is the only reason I am here even asking for my benefits is ballsy. I know that's how it likely would happen without the context of my issues with the state.

In the months since the initial Stay-At-Home orders last spring, many companies had different things that they had to do to help customers despite the limitations that COVID-19 brought them. Walmart, of course, closed at 6 pm for a few months, which was weird. They mentioned that it was for "enhanced cleaning and sanitizing to help prevent the spread of COVID-19". Last week, I went to Walmart near my house to get a couple of items, and I saw a half-eaten chicken drumstick on the shelf with the sodas, dead flies by the self-checkout, and a syringe near the bench outside the store.

How's that cleaning going for you? They close at 11 pm now, so does that mean they aren't cleaning as much? If someone were to call them out on what I saw publicly in a news story about unclean Walmart stores, despite closing overnight for cleaning and sanitizing measures, I am sure some corporate PR spin artist would say something like:

(Again, a parody, except the chicken, flies, and syringe were real)

"We regret the issues that were brought to our attention at the Walmart on Rinconada in Las Cruces, NM. Because of the extraordinary toll COVID-19 has taken on all of us, including staffing for our 10,000 locations, we regret that we missed a few things and regret the poor customer experience. We worked throughout the pandemic to provide a top-notch customer service experience and will always do so. We will learn from this and continue to do better."

According to Walmart's website, they employ 2.3 million people. They hired my mom and dad, and my first cousin is still a big-time manager of a store. (Shit, I better not say her name) They can't clean better until this happens?

Even a company like Walmart with more resources than God himself would stoop so low as to blame COVID-19 for piss-poor service.

Big banks helped their customers by closing many locations in major metropolitan areas at the onset of the pandemic. They did this not to limit the spread of COVID-19 because what ended up happening is that everyone that banked at a closed branch just went to a branch that was open and made that one 10x as busy. That likely increased the chances of infection in my mind.

Banks did that to push their digital banking methods and self-service options so they could tell their shareholders that their record profits were because of a "mass digital migration by our clients to our app and ATM self-service options." This will inevitably lead to fewer teller jobs and worse service over time. I know about this because I lost my job because of this lie.

When COVID-19 eased up slightly in the fall of 2020, some Wells Fargo and Bank of America locations were STILL closed, despite no capacity limits in some cities. Locations were closed in areas with no extreme mandates. Local news stations across the country took notice, partly because of my work gathering and promoting clients' voices affected by this.

Per an article from The Eastsider LA, a local media company in California, a reporter ran a story nine months after COVID-19 first hit about why some Bank of America branches in a predominantly Mexican-American neighborhood were STILL closed when banks all around BofA were open.

(This isn't a parody, sadly)

"We continue to take several steps to support our clients and employees during the health crisis, including some temporary financial center closures. Our temporary financial center closures have occurred in areas where we're seeing fewer visits; where a smaller location may be close to a larger location that is better able to accommodate physical distancing; or when our staffing is not sufficient for all to remain open (for example, if employees find themselves needing to take time off to care for family members or if someone becomes high risk due to a preexisting condition). Please know that when a center closes we work to reopen it as soon as possible.

So...they blame it on square footage. A building they chose to lease or buy is now the problem. Instead of limiting the number of people in the branch to scale it to meet social distancing, they close the branch and send at a minimum of 4,000 clients (what my small branch had) to a bigger bank who in turn cannot handle the surge? It's fucking ridiculous.

Then the coup de grace of blaming it on their associates and their (potentially) sick family members. Look, I am all for helping out our fellow man here, but I worked for this company. I once didn't take lunch for three months when a fellow banker quit because low-level managers are graded on their "forecast adherence." In layman's terms, if they say you need three employees at 9 am, you better staff three at 9 am, or it can impact your performance assessment. I couldn't leave to eat. If I did, then myself, my boss, and the branch gets a red mark for that. Considering the push to deemphasize branch services, it's funny how they hold your feet to the fire on that issue.

The public doesn't know that they will move heaven and earth to comply with the forecast adherence, up to and including borrowing associates from other centers to satisfy a regional manager. So that is a lie as well. Managers are resourceful, as are their superiors making sure that someone above them both doesn't horn in on their day-to-day.

I want to stop talking about COVID-19 for a second, even though this is the only reason this book exists to make my point another way. For those of you that don't know me, first, thank you for buying this book. I am eating healthy tonight because of you. Secondly, I love some analogies. I was raised on the humor of Dennis Miller and George Carlin, and telling stories with humor is an effective way of reaching an audience. So here goes.

I fucking love the Food Network show, "Restaurant Impossible." I do for a lot of reasons, first, Robert Irvine and his physique. He gives me something to strive for in my 50s, and if I am half as buff as him, I would be happy. Secondly, I love the sob stories people give about their failing restaurant to Robert, and he just cuts through their bullshit with surgical precision.

Pre-Pandemic, most restaurant owners told the same lie about why their restaurant was failing for ten years. One of the last episodes that aired in 2020 pre-COVID had a gentleman with an Italian restaurant in West Virginia (That's the reason why they are failing) on the program. Robert barges in, and the owner goes to shake his hand.

Now comes the made-for-TV moment. Robert asks them why they think they are failing. This guy had his story all prepared in his head, waiting for Robert to lend a sympathetic ear.

"Well, when we opened in 2006, the lines were out the door. We were so busy, making money hand over fist. I was hiring a lot more staff to help us with the surge in customers. Unfortunately, 2008 came, and the recession caused the customers to stop coming in as much, and we haven't recovered since."

Robert interrupts him and says what's on his mind, and frankly, my mind as well. As of the recording of this episode, the recession happened 11 years ago. How are you still using that as an excuse? If your excuse for failure were a human being, it would be in middle school now. That's how old the excuse is.

I am 36 years old watching this show, and I am laughing. He is using an excuse for something that happened when I was 25 years old. I was picking up dates on Myspace...MYSPACE in 2008 when his turning point occurred in his business. I was binge-drinking at college parties. The turning point came, and it's been a lot of straightaways since, my friend.

Look, I am not here to question the restaurant owner that 2008 didn't impact him. I am sure it did in some way. But the fact that he was around for 11 years afterward tells me that he overcame that to some extent in some way. Instead of blaming 2008, he could say, "I survived a recession, and for 11 years, we have tried to get back to our old glory. But we failed. We need help."

Honesty is the best policy. Honesty can be brutal, but it can open doors.

As I said, though, I am no excuse maker, and although I was one as a young kid, I have learned from those days and have used my failures then as a guide for making sure people are treated equally and fairly in customer service bank situations with my project. I don't want to hear or expect to hear an excuse from the NMDWS for why my unemployment claim got ignored, then denied for inexplicable reasons.

One of my favorite pro wrestlers used to say, "Don't break your arm patting yourself on the back too much." I think society does that in times of crisis. When we work as hard as we do, we expect a few certainties in our day. It's only normal. When someone or something like COVID-19 or 9/11 or whatever tries to shoehorn into someone's routine, people get flustered, of course, and that is why I can understand the stress levels of someone fielding calls for a state unemployment department. But after weathering an insane wave, shouldn't you be BETTER at your job and not shittier because of less volume, more attention to pay to individuals and the fact that you impressed yourself by helping God knows how many thousands of customers?

Don't you want to take pride in that? I thought overcoming obstacles to help people also means that you can't fucking also use it as a crutch to be bad, lazy, or apathetic. Imagine learning how to read when you are 30, and at 35, you get in a car accident. You forgot to yield. The police officer mentions to you that you not yielding is what caused the accident. You then say to the cop, "Well, you know I overcame a lot of obstacles in my life. I learned how to read at age 30, and have been only reading for five years, so that's why I didn't see that sign."

Will that hold up? I thought not.

The long and short of it is I have seen NMDWS and the State of New Mexico led by Governor Michelle Lujan Grisham pat themselves on the back a lot during COVID-19. Despite hearing a million insane people calling her tons of names, I believe she has done an excellent job the last couple of years, despite the circumstances. You can't blame the pilot for turbulence in the air, and you can't blame the events of COVID-19 and how it crept in your life on her or any leader for that matter.

But despite that endorsement right now, I have seen many people with horror stories about their unemployment benefits in New Mexico in the last year. If the media doesn't amplify the issues, someone like Ricky Serna or Governor Grisham would not likely hear about it.

A state is like any big company. There are managers for a manager's manager's manager. There is someone whose sole job is to take care of things, so the people above them don't have to. I know how it works. But as this whole chapter outlines...It's no excuse not to help someone.

AN OPEN LETTER TO THE HATERS

This is a letter to the people who rail against unemployment benefits, saying that they are the reason "no one wants to work anymore." This is a letter to people who mock people receiving those benefits and think they are getting a windfall and not still barely scraping by if they are lucky. This is a letter to those who laugh and mock without ever talking to someone who needs help. This is for you.

First off, if you hate "government handouts," and you bought this book that rails against the system that screwed me over and it's a lot of pages ranting about why I didn't get my government handout, thank you. You are a bigger person than I thought you were. I agree that this situation here is weird, but I am confident we can find some common ground. Let me help you understand where I come from and let me try to understand why you think everyone wanting money is a worthless bum.

You are a good person, deep down. I know it.

So, you are talking to a man who grew up with people on both sides of the aisle politically. No, I am not going to talk politics in this book that way, but I want to say that I have voted for people on both sides, and I have had family run for public office with both an R and a D attached to their name. I am married to a person who hails from "We voted for Trump by sixty percentage points" territory, and I have lived in two college cities in my life, bastions of liberal thinking. I got a healthy dose of this as a kid, and at age 38, I am pretty much done with it.

I can tell you that election week 2020 made me physically ill. Not because of who won or lost. I really stopped caring. It was mainly because of the intensity of that week in general. My blood pressure was too high to donate plasma because of the nonstop viewing of election coverage and the social media vitriol. I was immersed in it. Combining that with my line of work being an advocate for people with banking issues, I was around a lot of high-volume stress that week. I tuned out after that. I just had to. Social media nearly drove me insane.

As I write this, I am 3 days removed from the "60 Minutes" interview with the Facebook whistleblower who claims that the social network's algorithm is tailored to induce activity by its users. Meaning? Stories are fed to you to piss you off and get you thinking bad about the world more and more. I am truly a believer in that because of COVID-19, the elections, and everything in between.

Working as a banker on the "bad side of town," I saw people with money struggles every day. I saw the cliché thing you may have heard about: an older person having to choose whether to eat or buy a prescription. I witnessed people assessed a $35 fee by the bank for how an auto-debit out of their hands settled in the account creating a negative balance.

Things like that never leave you. I used to think only the worst about homeless and needy people until I got to meet and help a few. (I regularly donate to a food bank despite my lack of money recently, FYI) I used to be on welfare as a kid, and I know how it feels, so when I see a family pay shifty-eyed because they think they are being judged at the store with an EBT card (Food Stamps) which my high school idiot friends used to call "Eat Better Tonight Card," I don't judge. I understand.

I have seen single moms with car notes with 19% interest rates because their ex-husband fucked their credit, they work two jobs to support their kids, and 60% of their income goes to rent and daycare when housing should account for no more than 28% of your income. When your bank advertises a 1.99% special refinance rate to save money, and that woman comes there with a gleam in their eye, and you tell them you can't help them because the bank doesn't think they are a good credit "risk" (I hate that word), it affects you.

So, I have no qualms about anyone getting "Stimmy"

money, extended unemployment benefits if they lost their job or any other benefit that came from the pandemic. You shouldn't either. Let me be a little harsh before I try to find peace with you.

With every login to Facebook, I always get the "Unemployment went up" or "Unemployment went down" story on whatever news organization is posting that. I stopped reading the comments last year. I just look on the bottom left-hand corner to see the emojis, and there are always 100 reactions, and half of them are laughing emojis as if to say that these people's "life event" (That's bank speak) is fucking hilarious shit. That's bullshit.

I grew up with a lot of you so-called tough guys in my life. The same people would say, "Fire me? Fuck you, I quit." when they get into it with their boss. The same people will refuse to go to the doctor unless they are dying. The same type of people never show emotion because it's a sign of weakness. But to laugh at someone's issue and know that several million people almost had no way to pay the bills or eat? That's fucked up.

People like that either have spent their life avoiding emotions from everyone for their selfish reasons, or they have never been around scenes that I've seen from childhood onto my career. It's unimaginable what happened in 2020, and I pray it never happens again, just so I never have to see how heartless people are.

I see posts about the number of COVID-19 deaths and cases. You get laughing emojis there too. It has become a Tik Tok society where context is missing, and people consume information in short bursts without the backstory. That's what is wrong.

One of the most significant issues I had with working as a "Relationship Manager" at the bank was that the training to be a relationship manager taught you to think in generalizations. That all customers have the exact basic needs, and here are the products we can sell them. I learned in this state, that's not how it works.

I had day laborers as customers who got paid weekly, usually by some old farmer who "liked to write out his checks by hand and sign them personally." Oh, that's cute. Your employee will pay this bank $144 this year because my bank decided to punish this person for having a job with an old, set-in-his-ways boss. Thank you, sir.

You tell that to someone higher up than you, and we would get a, "Well, sometimes there's nothing you can do in that situation, unfortunately." Apathy like that leads to careless attitudes about people starving and struggling. I had customers who would get hit with $2.50 "out of network fees" for checking their balance to take money out possibly. Despite the fact, the ATM said: "Free Balance Inquiry" (Screw You, Murphy USA), they meant that THEY wouldn't charge you, not your bank. So, the client would have $21.00, check their balance, and then at that point have $18.50, and they can't take it out because it's a $20 minimum.

Do you know who checks their balance? People with little to no money!

That's likely half of the people who laugh at others' misfortunes on social media, and that's what pisses me off. Poverty and people struggling are both systemic and systematic. It's systemic in the sense that everywhere someone who struggled during this pandemic faced a fucking hurdle. Whether it was at their job, the unemployment office, the bank that was charging them for not having direct deposit, their landlord who was giving them shit because of the eviction freeze, it all worked together to break these people.

It's systematic in the sense that everything that seemingly happened bad at all those stops was so methodical in causing issues for these people. Many lower-end jobs, i.e. a local restaurant, aren't going to have a three-person HR staff trying to locate the workers they laid off during COVID-19. They will try to reload their roster without really trying to reach out to old workers. They move on. Trust me. I have an aunt that owns a prominent burger joint in NM. She could be ruthless at times.

Unemployment has these fucking archaic forms and

weirdly worded questions that make it inevitable that someone will mess up or not understand what's being asked. I am a college graduate, and I felt dumb trying to navigate that myself. If what was said in my denial letter is accurate, not knowing how to fill out a form appropriately is NOT an excuse.

With banks… Oh god, with banks. Methodical is the simplest way to put how someone who makes minimum wage pays more to the bank in fees than someone with $200k and 20 high-end checking accounts. My former bank changed the rules from "Any direct deposit" to "At least a $250 minimum direct deposit" to avoid a monthly fee. It also changed balance requirements from "Average Daily Balance of $1,500" to "Minimum Daily Balance of $1,500". The new condition pretty much says to someone making minimum wage that you have to keep about six weeks of pay in here, or we will take the equivalent of a week of income from you a year just for fucking breathing here.

Finally, let's talk about the landlord's situation with the eviction freezes. Say someone cannot pay rent, but the landlord can't kick them out. What do you think happened in a lot of instances? Resentment, anger, possible harassment. I am sure hundreds of thousands of times throughout the pandemic, landlords said either under their breath or out loud, "This bitch owes me money."

People under stress like that cannot cite the federal eviction moratorium from the CDC. I know some landlords that can barely read and write in my home state. They don't know what the CDC is, and they don't know what the word moratorium is. Their friend tells them, "That means you can't kick the freeloaders out."

"Why not? That dumb bitch owes me two months' rent."

I hate using language like that, but you've got to understand that when people don't know how this works and why it's done, you tend to be crankier about it than usual. While I don't blame certain "mom and pop landlords" for being mad because they weren't getting money, everything done was for the bigger picture.

Now, if you disagree with me, let me ask you something. Do you think that state unemployment benefits were a financial windfall for people who lost their jobs, making them not want to go back? Let me fact-check you.

In New Mexico, the maximum state benefit you can get is $433 a week pre-tax, which is $10.82 an hour if you worked 40 hours. Let's say you got laid off from a job that pays $20 an hour, like my last stint in banking. How much did I get? $10.82 an hour from the state in unemployment. That's half. Could you survive on half your pay?

Also, let's remember that I said MAXIMUM benefit. That doesn't mean you qualify for it all. Your pay and time put in have to calculate to that number.
In Florida, it's $275 a week, which is the equivalent of $6.87 an hour, less than the federal minimum wage. Have you been to Florida? It's a little pricey. Again, that's the MAXIMUM benefit if you qualify. Most got less. Who knew New Mexico would beat Florida in something? Not everyone got the same thing in different parts of this great country of ours.

The $600 a week windfall that people got in Spring 2020 sounds delicious as hell, right? In the best-case scenario, let's say someone like me could bank a little money because I have a low cost of living and an insanely low mortgage payment. Worst case scenario? You still took a loss and are still in arrears with rent/mortgage and possibly other bills. And NO, that housing payment you missed won't be forgiven. You WILL have to pay that back eventually.

Is that the hill you want to die on believing people got it made?

Now, I will give you this. Yes, some people take advantage of the systems meant to help people. I told you, I saw people selling food stamps as a kid. I have seen a few of my bank coworkers falsify their bank statements to get subsidized child care because they had no help from others. I knew someone 20 years ago who used the unemployment insurance he got from being fired as a janitor to buy marijuana to sell it.

Cannabis is a crop that will soon be legal in my state. Still, at the time, this person was looking to find a steady way to feed his family and continue to live in a neighborhood of my hometown in Socorro, NM, affectionately known as Stinky Acres.

Why do they call it Stinky Acres? Because it's a trailer park next to the sewage plant. Every trailer I have ever been in at Stinky Acres smells like raw sewage. They routinely have roaches and mice in their houses. This is real life, and it's real-life that is met with a chuckle back home, instead of disgust for a system that allows a trailer park to smell like shit 24/7/365. He WANTED to protect his home AT STINKY ACRES!

I get why you use those examples for why people shouldn't get help. But it goes the same way. If you are of the conservative persuasion, which I have friends that identified as for a long time, and your thing is guns, family, and American pride, I can understand that. I'm from New Mexico. Guns are a way of life with hunting here. Family is everything to us. American pride is almost as great here as anywhere because half the country doesn't realize we're a state.

Would you want to be lumped in with the worst from your side? (I'm not taking sides here, just asking a question.) No? Of course not. You and your family do you, live life and prosper, and don't blatantly hate someone seeking help without knowing why they are doing it and understanding their situation. I will give you an itemized list in a bit of what New Mexico will screw me out of if my unemployment doesn't pay me my money.

This book is a byproduct of COVID-19 as well. Yes, there will be a vast cottage industry of idiots like me writing books about what we all went through to make a few bucks and feed our families. Do you consider that work? Or am I still lazy because I am writing these words on my computer without wearing a shirt? Do I have to wear a shirt for it to be considered work? Ok, one sec, I'll be right back.

The truth is, it's not really about the "handouts" at all,

right? For a lot of you blue-collar, "Git R Done" folks, it's about your perception that this person did not work as hard as you did to get the money. I used to get that shit all the time when I worked at the bank.

"Must be nice to sit on your ass all day and count money."

Do you know how wrong you are? I was judged on my job performance HOURLY, and if I had a couple of bad days in a row, my work ethic was questioned. Counting money sucks. It takes forever, it hurts your wrists, and if you are of 0.001% from your computer's total for your vault, you are fired.

Only time I used to drink was when I got home because I was so mentally drained from the rat race that was the banking industry. Because of a few incidents at work, I even contemplated taking my life a time or two. Stress was real and all the time.

But because I didn't do something that required a CDL, heavy lifting, or breaking a sweat, then I am not holding a candle to your perception of EARNED money. I did sweat in my polyester pants a time or two. I am a big guy, and big guys sweat, you know, but that's not what you mean. Jobs are always about hierarchy or perceived hierarchy on some great list of complex jobs somewhere.

Waitresses? They have it easy, right? How about they are on their feet all day, make $2.13 an hour, and will make less than their worth because of shit tippers, and they get yelled at for mistakes in cooking when they are the ones just handing the food to someone.

Bartenders? They make great money. It must be easy to work in a bar and be around partying all the time, right? How about those people who are yelled at by customers regularly, and in the case of female bartenders, sexually harassed? They have to clean up your spilled drink, keep tabs on dozens of people from being overserved, and also have to manage hundreds of cash and card transactions amidst all the chaos. Oh, and they must make sure to balance their drawer at the end of the long night.

You know most of those people were out of work, too,

right?

You missed those places when they were closed to customers, right?

Do you realize your comments are technically directed at those people you couldn't live without and fought like hell for with a bunch of faceless social media commenters when there were stay-at-home orders?

I have a person who has bullied me for over 20 years, and it's still going on today. He's still on my ass about my former career, my current advocacy project, and all the things I try to do to make the world a better place. Nothing I have achieved has finally made him content with my choices because I will always be that "little bitch from school that thinks he's better than us because he writes books." This is a phrase I heard multiple times.

Whether or not I think I am better than anyone is something that I must look at myself in the mirror about at the end of the day. Still, I know my heart, and to the person who reads this and may not agree with "handouts", I can tell you the reason I addressed you is that even though you may not agree with things like this all the time, I am going to respect your point of view because you are allowed to have it. All I can do is show my cards to you in the hopes I can at least get you to say, "I understand."

The world would be a better place if we took the time to not talk in soundbites or what our friends want us to say, open our minds up, and understand there's a world beyond the bubble we are stuck inside. Aside from reaching out to people with bank issues, I don't want people in my house, nor do I want to invite people in the future in my house. I am a homebody, I keep to myself, and I want to live the best, most efficient life I can. I know that is what you want too. Just because your footsteps aren't following mine doesn't mean we both don't want to get to the same destination.

Thanks for your time,
James A. Baca

"The Notorious Banker"

I know many people who disagree with pandemic-based relief will not read this open letter to them. If I am lucky enough to get publicity on this book, I will check out social media. Some news organizations will post the headline, "New Mexico Man Writes Book as Payback For State Incorrectly Denying Unemployment to Him," on Facebook. It will have 100s of reactions, and half will be laughing emojis. There will be comments calling me an idiot, not realizing that this book IS work. I AM WORKING as I am creating a product to sell for money and still find a way to demean me and others who struggled in 2021.

I will see those posts, and I won't even look at the reactions/comments. I will simply exit out of whatever social media platform I am on, except for Twitter, which is project-related, and I will uninstall the fucking app from my phone. I tried to talk to you haters heart to heart, and you will still hate.

From a man who has had the internet for a quarter-century now, I can reluctantly say I was one of the first social media trolls out there at one point in my life. This time, I will be adult enough not to say anything back. Although I will mutter in my head, "Grow the FUCK up!!!"

DONATING PLASMA AND THE BATTLE TO STAY SOLVENT WHILE WAITING -- HOW I HAVE ALWAYS BEEN RESILIENT

I want to make it clear before I start going deep in this chapter. I am the BIGGEST cheerleader for donating blood plasma than anyone I know. I have been donating off and on for 19 years, and it got me to financial goals, kept me honest about my financial goals in my 20s, and now is a significant part of what I am doing to survive at 38 years old. I love being a part of the plasma donating process, and frankly, I should be a paid endorser for any of the major plasma centers nationwide. I will tell you why in a bit.

One thing I always knew about myself was that I was resourceful. Call me MacGuyver with money. I can make money stretch like silly putty because it was my job to think about money for years. I can make money stretch because we didn't have a lot of it when I was a child.

My family would go school clothes shopping at Family Bargain Center, which was three steps below Walmart on the hierarchy of quality products. It seriously made the clothes at Family Dollar look like Armani. It was rough times, but we survived it, save from getting bullied at school. I learned the hard numbers of what my mom earned, what it cost to "keep the lights on" at our trailer and live a normal (what we thought was normal anyway) life.

That hard reality of being poor young hits harder when you know what's going on behind the scenes with your elders, and the one thing I learned is that you don't quit. Ever. There have been some questionable/unethical things that both my mom did for us as kids and I did for myself as I came of age.

My mom would sneak a grilled cheese and fries out from work every night when she left. As I got older, it would be a burger or chicken sandwich. Yes, it was my Aunt's restaurant, but it was an aunt by marriage to my mom, and they didn't have the best relationship when my parents divorced.

As I got older, I became aware that the nicer things we had at home resulted from drug proceeds from my then-stepdad. What was I going to do? Call the cops on my stepdad and, in turn, ruin my life more? Give me a break. We were fine.

I started being rebellious when I was a freshman in High School, and I was truant a lot, causing many problems at home. I was acting out. I was mad about who knows what, but I sold the shit out of it, even getting the authorities involved. I was kicked out of high school, and I saw at 14 years old that the state of New Mexico doesn't have a safety net for some kids because I saw the powers that be not give a shit that I wasn't in school. Chalk that up to apathy at other departments in the state, but 14 years old could have been my educational end. It wasn't.

Around that time, I figured it out and decided to speed up my maturation process and go back to school on my timetable. My mom had a hands-off approach with me. She told me she didn't trust me, and I would have to pay my way to buy clothes or anything else I needed. I had a roof over my head, but I was not going to get any other extras.

So, I was too young to work, and I didn't have a car. I didn't know where I would start when it came to earning money, so I got online and logged into eBay for the first time. With the novelty of the auction site still fresh in the late 1990s, I used my above-average writing skills to hype up and sell a huge chunk of my possessions that I no longer wanted or needed. I sold clothes that were not fitting, and I spent hours perfecting the art of the sales pitch before I knew how to sell.

With a vast sports cards collection, old tennis gear from the one sports team I made, and with confidence in my words, I made about $5,000 at age 15 in a few months, three years before

I was technically allowed to be on eBay. Shh… don't tell anyone.

It was a big confidence boost because I figured out self-efficiency early on. As I got older and started driving to school and becoming savvier with how the world functions, I looked for the next idea to make money. Baseball cards were one thing, but how can I make real money while pursuing my high school diploma?

This was the era when DVDs were still a new thing. I had gone by the local university to illegally download some songs and burn them on a CD when I saw their computer lab had the first-ever DVD duplicator I had ever seen. I was in awe of this new technology. I had visions of what I could use that for and how I could use it to make money.

I had a side hustle of selling burned CDs on my home computer to my friends without computers for the cost of $1/song (I was a real-life iTunes). I would make hundreds of dollars a week dedicating my time to burning CDs while I studied. I thought nothing of what I did, although the music labels would have hated my guts and likely do now for even telling this story —but seeing that DVD duplicator gave me next-level vibes.

One of the trends I saw on eBay was selling TV series as a package on VHS or DVD. It seems funny to talk about it now, but box sets of shows were NOT a thing in 1999. Binge-watching was not yet a part of our lexicon. There were a lot of popular shows that were not for sale in stores. They were only available by appointment viewing on TV. Nowhere else. I had the bright idea to invest a little bit of money to make a lot of money doing what no one else did.

A cousin and I dropped $1000 on a DVD recorder, DVD Duplicator, and 4 VCRs to duplicate tapes. We were going to sell bootleg videos. Don't act as if you have never been to a flea market before. It's still a lucrative market out there. I am not a part of it now.

Anyway, spending a considerable chunk of my life savings proved to pay off, and I would sell episodes of shows, just one one-hour episode for $10 and a 13-episode season for $99. I made five figures on eBay at 16 years old, and no one, not even my mom, knew about it. It was a move that kept me surviving.

I know you are wondering why I didn't just get a burger-flipping job at that point. I was trying to make four years of credits in 2 ½ years because I screwed up as a freshman, and I flunked out technically. I had no time to myself, and I studied for hours at a time, which was reflected by my having no social life until college.

But blah blah blah I was resourceful. I saw the resourcefulness of my grandmother at an early age. She was an aluminum can picker while walking down the streets in Socorro. She would round up the cans and then run the cans over with her Ford, bag them, and reap the profits. A few extra dollars here and there by basically doing something no one else was doing. It was smart. She made wind chimes out of some of the cans, giving me vibes of Aunt Meg in the movie "Twister." It takes thinking outside the box sometimes to succeed, even in poverty.

Now, let's talk about plasma. I knew nothing of plasma donating at first. I had no clue of what it entailed or how to get started. They were just the people with the big ad in any alternative weekly paper in every big city. I used to pick up those papers to see what concerts were coming and what porn stars would be dancing at the local Gentlemen's club. But I was oblivious to it until fate kind of brought me to a donating center.

It was 2003. My bootleg DVD outfit had run its course because many of the shows I would bootleg were available now on DVD...Legit DVD. Weirdly, I like to think my family member and I are the reason you got those DVD sets in the store and get the entire series on streaming services. We realized a market was there, took advantage of it, and woke up an entire industry.

I was running a little short on money in the spring. I had worked an odd job here and there, but nothing too serious. My cousin Ramon had gotten a job with a company called Tresco here in Southern NM, which maintained the rest areas on I-25 and helped people with disabilities train for employment. It was a great company, as they employed a lot of my family members over the years. He was 21 years old, yet a little scared to go to a strange city (My current hometown of Las Cruces) and train with people he didn't know. I swear, my family is all the same in the sense that they are afraid of what they didn't know. That's why I didn't have Thai food until my late 20s.

Anyway, he wanted me to go with him to Las Cruces for three weeks to stay with him during his training. We were going to stay at a high-end motel, a Best Western, which was nice then, but now it's a shitty "America's Value Inn," he would get a healthy per diem for food as well. We would have pizza almost every day. Plus, the selling point was that I got to borrow his car, which I believe was an old Dodge Dart, for 9 hours a day to do whatever. I agreed. It sounded like fun, and I would get a chance to learn about this town which eventually became my home.

We go down to Las Cruces. It's April 2003. We check into the hotel, and we have a blast: No gangsta parties or illegal stuff. Just two cousins, practically brothers, having a good time and talking about life. We had access to the pool, which consisted of my cousin swimming in his damn fubu pants that weighed 10lbs and an oversized T-Shirt. I think a lot of New Mexicans can imagine the visuals. Ha. I had a blast.

Only problem? I didn't know what the hell to do throughout the day. Las Cruces is excellent, but it can teeter on boring if you don't have friends or hobbies. So, I go to a gas station to get a drink and pick up the Alternative Weekly paper. I believe it was called "What's Up" over here. I thumb through it and saw an ad for a plasma center here in town. It was advertising that a new donor could earn $200 for their first five donations.

$200? Wow, it sounded like a good deal to me. I was kind of afraid of needles at the time, but the way I saw it, this is money I can use to do something I wanted to do for a long, long time. Do you know what it was? Don't laugh, ok?

I wanted to get my nipples pierced, along with several facial piercings. Haha, yes, it's true. I was quite the metalhead at the time. Black t-shirts and gelled up spiky hair were my style. I was the envy of every Hot Topic cashier at the time. But I didn't have any tattoos, nor wanted any, but I wanted piercings. So, I decided on a whim to give plasma to earn this money. The five donations would be over three weeks. I would stay there with my cousin, and when I return home, I would go to Albuquerque to get them all done. I had a coupon. (I am an avid couponer to this day)

I walk into the center, and it sort of resembles a bus station waiting area. A lot of sullen faces waiting their turn to get screened. They would weigh you in public in those times like you were some animal or something. Very weird. I had to fill out a questionnaire and get physically screened. There was a problem once I got to the part where they were documenting IDs, and it became one of the first times I played the role of consumer advocate.

I lived too far away. They said my license, which said "Socorro, NM," was out of their range to accept me as a client. With the hopes of getting body pierced fading, I asked exactly how they came to that conclusion. They told me that I had to live 150 miles from the donation center, and according to their legend, they used to calculate the distance between NM towns, Socorro, NM was 152 miles away. I am not kidding.

The problem? I always knew Socorro to be 147 miles away. Socorro is exit 150 on I-25, and the exit to take to get to the plasma donating center was exit 3. You do the math. The doctor in charge said, "Why would the map lie?". I asked him what kind of map they had. They used a map you would see in a 70s-era gas station telling you the distance to the next stop. It was for an old truck stop off the last exit of Las Cruces, which was exit 1 and a few miles down the road from the I-10 entrance. So that's where they got 152 miles.

This was before the era of GPS on our phones, where I could navigate anywhere on a whim and get you hard numbers. So, I asked nicely if they could fire up Mapquest on their computer and plug in the center's address to my address. The person reluctantly agreed. 148.2 miles. HAHA! I win. Even if

I didn't donate, I was proven right. The doctor in charge said, "Well, that's good enough for me," and I continued the process of being onboarded to donate.

When I finally got in that bed, I started to get a little nervous, just like many people who have to do anything medically. My fears were calmed by a very excellent phlebotomist who had a tattoo of lips on his neck and talked to me about sports. As the first needle entered my arm, I cringed, but after a while, I turned my attention to watching the movie "The Wash" with Snoop Dogg and Dr. Dre on a TV they had set up.

After four subsequent donations, my time in Las Cruces ended, and I got my $200 banked for my piercings. It was one of very few trips out of Socorro I did as an adult, and I had so much fun getting away from the malaise of back home. It was also my first venture into making a secondary income that was not illegal or against the rules.

Just to let you all know, I did get all the piercings I wanted, except my nose (septum), because they were out of the jewelry for that piercing. I still have the nipple piercings to this day. I had a couple of eyebrow piercings ripped out at a metal concert when I had a skirmish in the mosh pits, and the last one I took out after getting hired at Bank of America. The true gift in all that was learning about plasma donating. I knew that it was easy money and helping save lives, as a lot of their advertising will tell you. I encourage you to read up on it.

It also stoked the fires of me wanting to leave my hometown and grow my career. Cut to 2008, and I wanted to move away from Socorro. If not for the rampant drug use and petty crimes impacting my town, I would have been fine in my little rut. But those issues were affecting my family and me directly. I wanted to go far away and see new things and meet new people.

I met an employee from BofA in Las Cruces while working in Socorro. She was there to fill in for a manager. She and I became friendly, and eventually, she allowed me to use her as a reference to transfer to her branch as they needed experienced senior tellers there. The only issue was, I was not going to be promised 40 hours all the time. The most they could give me was 30 max. I needed a way to fill the gaps for the 10 hours I'm losing so I can pay rent and the bills.

This was when Bank of America claimed to be a great place to work for students. They used to work around your schedule and were very flexible with you when I was in school. In late 2008, as the recession and all the bailout bullshit happened, it was no longer the case. They grew cold over there, so I wasn't allowed to work a second job to supplement my income while at BofA, so I decided there would be one thing I could do to help me pay the bills.

Plasma.

I got to see my old friends at the plasma center. I calculated the maximum I'd make a month donating regularly. It was more than I would make working ten more hours at Bank of America. Back then, the company that ran the plasma center paid cash, so I wasn't taxed on it like at work. Trust me, many people who donate aren't thinking about their taxes. They are just worried about paying bills.

In 5 years, I had evolved from a metalhead looking to make money to have metal shot through his body to a struggling professional looking to supplement income while working his way up the corporate ladder. It was funny to go into the center in a full suit every day. Most of the people who donated were blue-collar types, so I found another way to stick out…again. I would lay in my bed, undo my shirt cuff, roll up my sleeve, and be in and out in about an hour. I typically do it after my shifts at work, just because I am always a little tired after donating.

For two years, I went to donate regularly. Yes, I have a tiny scar on my right arm, my preferred arm for donating, but I don't think about it. It's a sign that I did what I could to make sure I can continue to work hard to be a productive member of society and pay my bills. I knew that I wanted more with my career, but the most challenging thing climbing the BofA ladder was waiting for people to retire or leave to move up. A lot of people ahead of me were near my age, making things harder.

In late 2010, I got my first break at BofA. I got promoted to Sales and Service Specialist. It's a teller with sales goals. It would be a lot of stress, but it came with a $2 raise and a guarantee of 40 hours. I found out that when tellers or bankers quit, this meant that I would always have to cover their shifts, so it meant 5-7 hours of overtime every week at $18/hour. I was exhausted every day I had that role before my second promotion. The extra money was excellent. I had a little bit of money in the stock market at the time, and I made a huge investing gamble which doubled my savings. (Shout Out SIRI on the stock ticker)

This meant one thing, though. I had to say goodbye to the plasma center and regular donations. I just didn't have the time or the energy to do that. In retrospect, I should have made time. My girlfriend wasn't living here yet. (She later became my wife) I had no friends, aside from those at work, and I was just going home and watching ESPN. I could have bought a fucking car. Oh well.

I knew what I wanted, and I was getting it—money and being rewarded for working hard. I put in everything I had into being the best worker I could be. I wanted to be the face of Bank of America to the thousands of clients that showed up every month at my branch. There was always so much negativity with the company. I knew that if I made the experience mine, I could win over the trust of many skeptical customers. I did just that.

So, over the years, I grew into a management role at Bank of America. My fucking pathetic $8.50 an hour became $22 at the end. The only reason I say "pathetic" about that pay rate is not demeaning low-wage workers. It's just that I wouldn't accept $50/hour for it now because of the stress involved with that role. So many low-wage workers deal with that as well. I was able to pay my bills quickly, buy a house with my wife, and start an existence here in Las Cruces, NM, that was more "member of the community" instead of "a stepping stone to where I want to be."

Sitting behind a desk and talking to people about their

money in an area with very little of it gives you a new perspective on what people perceive as money problems. I've been called a "fucking asshole" by a person who owned three restaurants and was a millionaire because BofA charged him $5 for a copy of a statement he lost and needed a reprint.

I also have had hundreds of people beg me for money. Whether it was a refund on a fee that the bank erroneously charged or a small loan to cover rent (we don't do personal loans, only credit cards), or people who were on the streets asking for a buck as they passed us to get to the bus station across the street. These are things that happen daily.

If I had to estimate how many times I reached into my own pocket to help someone who asked for a buck or worse yet, how many times I paid someone's $35 overdraft fee that I couldn't refund for fear of getting fired, I would say I spent about $1500 of my own money doing that. I did the "pay the overdraft thing" at least 10-15 times. It was the right thing to do, and I wasn't going to let the bank hurt these people even more.

When I didn't do that, I would have long conversations, often to the detriment of being chewed out by my boss. These conversations were with people seeking help with figuring out their money and what little they had of it. I was a PERSONAL BANKER or a RELATIONSHIP MANAGER. While those titles are just sugary ways of saying, "I'm going to find a way to open up ten accounts for you," I took the titles literally. I wanted to help people think about their money.

So, I remember about 2012 or so. I helped this really tough guy. He had a tattoo on his bald head and his arms signifying a former life in gangs. We were cool, as I talked to him before. We had previously talked about the vintage Dallas Cowboys bobblehead in my office. This afternoon, he came in and asked if he could close the door. I said yes, although I knew I would get in trouble for this. Bank of America doesn't allow you to close doors when you have a client in there, lest you beat them up or vice versa.

So, I closed the door, and as I did, he was in the ugly

red chairs of the bank, crying his eyes out. He tells me that he needs a loan because they cut his hours at Olam, a factory that makes spices and constantly smells like a chile flavored potato chip outside. He doesn't know if he will be able to give his kids Christmas.

As he is telling me this, we are in October, which speaks to how the commercialization of Christmas impacts almost everyone, as this guy was crying about gifts two months out. There's something about men with tough exteriors (myself included) having to show toughness for so long until they finally have to emote in weird ways because they held it in too long. This guy likely went straight and found that getting a 9-5 and doing everything properly can still make you eat shit constantly. There are few winners in the rat race.

This is the first time I decided to use this suggestion to have a good Christmas for his kids. My training would tell me to offer him a Cash Rewards credit card where every purchase you make earns you 1% cashback, which means you will have more money for Christmas. No, fuck that. I mentioned to him, "Have you ever thought about donating plasma to supplement your income?"

I didn't know what his answer would be. I figured either "Yes" or "No."

Instead, I got, "What's plasma?"

My salesmanship kicked in a bit just because I wanted to make it sound like something that he really should do. I explained in detail what it entailed, the amount of time you would spend per donation, and how much monthly you made in a ballpark figure. I didn't know the exact amount then, but I DO know it was more than when I left, and they now give you a debit card.

The way I hyped it up turned his sad face into an optimistic one. It was cool. I got to see him motivated to get this done for his kids. He left straight to the center, which was about three blocks away from the bank. I felt like I did a good deed in helping him figure out a solution to the problem.

Around Christmastime that year, He went to the bank and gave the tellers and me candy canes. He told me privately that he saved $400 for Christmas and got his daughter, who was in high school at the time, a tablet. Couldn't afford an iPad, but something to help her with her studies, he proclaimed. I felt so good about that. More about him shortly.

So for the next 5.5 years, anytime people asked me quick ways to make easy money at the bank, I would joke, "Drugs, stripping, or plasma donating." People saw my lighthearted way of trying to brainstorm how to help people. Still, from the age of 10, talking with my mom about her bills and trying to survive, I had conversations almost every day about bettering people's financial lives.

Off the record, the two companies who owned the plasma donation center before the current one there should pay me about $10,000 in referral fees. I'm only half kidding, of course, but I know so many people who donate that were my clients to this day. Of course, the people get compensated for their time to donate, but I know that one donation of plasma can be sold for a high price, so I likely made them hundreds of thousands of dollars just by planting some seeds.

When I lost my job at Bank of America, it was 9:14 on a Friday in August. I didn't think it was coming, but I was not surprised at the same time. I got all my shit from the bank in a box and left out a back door, unable to say goodbye to my friends who worked with me for years. I was so sad driving out of that lot. All I remember was a song by Camila Cabelo in the background as I waited at a stoplight, and my brain went back into survival mode. My thoughts?

"I need to find my social security card, so I can donate plasma on Monday."

It was immediately back to the grind of trying to make things work out for ol' James. I resent a lot of how my time in banking ended, but at the same time, the work I have done since and the humbling I got have made me a better man. I am no man of faith, but I see a higher calling for me as I write this book, and

I struggle to fight for my money and figure out ways to make money.

I have donated plasma about 150 times since I left BofA. I will tell you that I have made over five figures in money donating. This has supplemented what I had, and frankly, allowed me to pursue my dream of helping people with financial problems. I am there to help people full-time because of donating plasma.

I would be destitute without plasma donating, and I think even if I landed a 6-figure job somewhere, I would still donate. I really would. It would be my car payment money. It's already my mortgage payment money as we speak.

So, a funny thing happened one Friday in November 2018 as I was waiting to donate. I usually go Thursdays and Saturdays, but because Thanksgiving was such an insanely busy day, I took the day off and decided to go the next day. I go through the screening, and when it's time to lay on a bed, I see a pair of eyes looking at me. I am wearing jeans and an NMSU t-shirt, and I don't look like the Calvin Klein suit-wearing banker people knew. I recognized him immediately because of his tattoos.

He says, "Hey, bro, did you used to work at The Bank of America?"

I said, "Yessir."

"Man, it's good to see you!" We shared a complicated handshake. It was fantastic to talk with someone who knew me from that world because I had mostly tried to hide from everyone since I left. He asks me if I still work at BofA since they closed the other one.

"No, man, they fired me. I do a podcast now, and I talk about bank news online, usually on Twitter to a lot of people." At this point, I had to tell him what a podcast was, much like me telling him what plasma donating was six years earlier. I told him how he could listen to it.

"Sounds good, man. I'll have my daughter help me find it when she gets back from school on her winter break. I don't know how to work this shit to find stuff."

So, his daughter was in college now? How awesome, and at the same time, what a way to make me feel old. I didn't ask, but I wondered if he was donating to help his daughter pay for school now? Was donating plasma a way to continue to supplement his income as he worked at several low-paying jobs? I didn't want to pry. It was not my job to pry anymore.

We talked for a little bit more, and his plasma donating is complete. He is waiting for the phlebotomist to disconnect him from the machine that draws out the plasma. He looks like he's in no hurry. He's chilling there watching a movie on a tablet...an old RCA brand tablet.

Hmm. Was that the tablet that he got his daughter years ago that propelled her to college? Sonofabitch, I'll never know, as I haven't seen him since that day, but I sure would love to believe that. How cool is that?

I had to have an ode to plasma donating because it has given me financial opportunities in different ways for different reasons over the years. I am a firm believer that it has a lot to do with my solvency then and now, and I can't be more thankful that we have a center in a small town like this where I can earn a good chunk of money.

I have had conversations with plasma companies about them sponsoring my projects, to little or no avail, because they don't know me from Adam at this point. This story I am telling you, coupled with the pull I had on my clients over the years, tells me that I am successful at referring, a word that Bank of America loves to use.

Salesmanship for something I don't have a direct financial stake in is proof that in a world often where people who need money aren't afforded a break, there are ways to give yourself a chance. I used to hear people say that plasma donating is good for "a little extra money in your pocket." I see it as bill money. I see it as money that will get you to a better place and help save lives. I see it as your chance to get the upper hand at the game of life.

I share this story to show you my resiliency and tell

you that because I always found a way to succeed whenever the chips are down, I will find a way to succeed in getting the unemployment owed to me by the state.

The scars of letting the State win by ignoring me will be more profound than any scar I have from a needle in my arm meant to draw blood out!

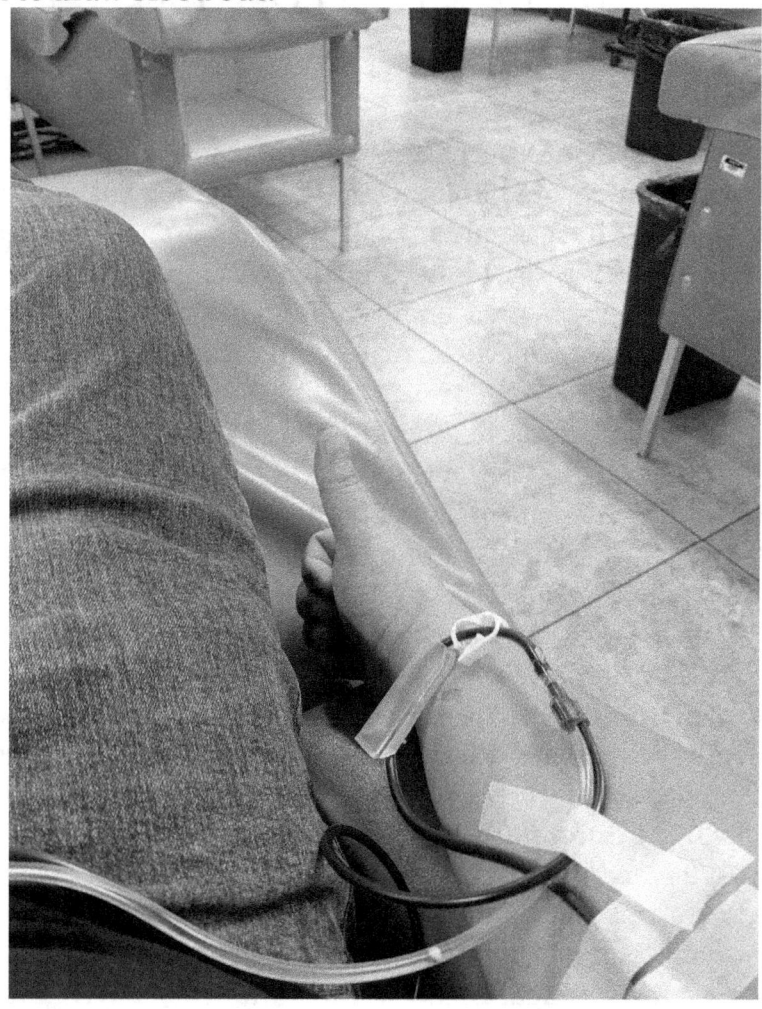

SEEING HOW STATES AND BANKS SYSTEMATICALLY KEPT PEOPLE FROM HELP

I'm despondent.

I had spent the better part of 3 years helping people fight back against big banks when they got burned on fees and fraud claims. I have made it my life's passion and the reason I get up in the morning. I have a purpose for the first time in my life, and every day brings a new challenge. Since COVID-19 hit, I struggled with finding the time to help myself, all while helping others.

Since this book is a byproduct of me putting in a lot of effort to get assistance and the State of New Mexico shitting the bed in helping me, I have had to dedicate a lot of time to figure it out. This means I am not helping as many people as I could in the meantime. Talk about a trickle-down effect.

My story of getting burned is FAR from a unique one. It is pretty standard. While I get that COVID-19 brought a lot of challenges for many entities, states and banks alike, the fact that problems still exist and we are seeing the people in charge start to inch away from the people who need help slowly is insane.

All the different relief programs that spawned because of COVID-19 blew my mind. My family member got 2x the amount of food stamps that she usually gets. I had an option to freeze my student loan payments. Some banks volunteered to let their clients go into forbearance for their monthly payments, with many of them not letting the clients know that it wasn't a gift and that they would have to eventually pay that off at a later date, with accrued interest.

Of course, we all knew about the Stimulus checks, the

unemployment benefits, and PPP Loans for small businesses. Many people were aware of them simply because the feds and the states helped promote these programs, making it almost impossible to avoid and seemingly way more user-friendly than it was.

So why have I spent over a year talking with reporters about the flaws that banks that were placed in charge to help with some of these programs not only didn't help people, it arguably puts a lot of small businesses out of business with their ineptitude and apathy?

I have had the good fortune of chatting with a few outstanding reporters in the last three years. A few of them are checking whether there is a good story with me, and a few are curious about this crazy guy talking about banking often on social media. I would be lying if I said this book isn't a byproduct of my overall media consumption and how they love to talk about stories like the one I am telling here.

From the first time a media story enthralled me, the 1995 OJ Simpson trial, I liked to see how the media ticked. I liked to understand how a story was reported and why it should be reported. A full quarter-century later, there were many angles to cover when it came to COVID-19, and I think one of the biggest things that the media didn't cover correctly was that a lot of big banks found a way to help as little as possible during the pandemic.

That's why I volunteered to help as many people as I could. When big banks shifted a lot of employees to work from home, I noticed a big difference in the quality of how someone was getting helped by the bank. Whether it was PPP Loans, questions with their unemployment cards, or just basic bank customer service, I saw more upset people than satisfied people online.

The Summer of 2020 was something else, though. I saw people trying to qualify for federal loan programs like PPP for small businesses get the old silent treatment from Wells Fargo and Bank of America. I saw people who poured everything into the American dream, only to see the bucket kicked over like the bank was some asshole kid while you are trying to build a sand sculpture.

Most people don't realize that big banks act as fiscal agents for many of these programs like unemployment and PPP loans during the pandemic. They were the subcontractors for the government. The government was like, "Take down these folks' info, and we will get you the money to give them."

Sounds easy enough, right? Before you agree with me, understand that banks don't see anything to gain from those transactions. For PPP, they saw it as "not their loan." They saw it as "Shit, we have a ton of extra work we don't want to do for people we don't care about." Why do they not care about them? Because they aren't going to be making much money off these things.

Most banks essentially got a finder's fee for helping people with PPP, but what happened was the money was not that life-altering for a bank, and some banks like Wells Fargo just gave it to charity. They gave money to help the same minority business owners who had a hard time through the loan process, so they gave to people they burned.

The people who applied for PPP Loans could never get a business loan at a big bank. I would know. As a personal banker, pretty much my job was to find qualified small business clients for loans. In 13 years of referring small businesses to loan products, I never had one business loan get funded by BofA. My clients' businesses were small potatoes to them. So, when the government says, "Hey, these nice people at the bank can help you out!" many don't realize the attitude a bank has about those clients. Mom forced them to be nice to you since everyone was getting sick, and you needed money.

For years, I was trained to have that attitude.

"What's in it for me to waste my time with these people?"

It's a very potent part of the toxic culture of banks. They don't think about helping people in the now for the sake of assisting in the now. Banks focus on what those companies can bring to them if they decide to help finally. If I help a business with 250 employees get a PPP loan, is it possible I can poach some employees to come bank with us so we can discuss their financial futures? It's all a play for getting the most out of as little work as possible.

I learned from a person I helped in Florida that Bank of America had its small business specialists pre-draft up some PPP Loan applications for their perceived top clients. This was to have them ready when the client comes in during that initial glut of applications. Big banks were allowed to set their guidelines of who to help, and Bank of America's original PPP guidelines effectively eliminated a lot of small-time business clients from even seeking an application during the first day.

Since I have about 5 million impressions a month on Twitter (@BankBetterGuy), I was not the most famous person by a long shot. Still, I had a lot of influence on carrying the conversations that were going on about Bank of America, so I shared my opinion on PPP guidelines the bank put up.

I ended up getting 10 Million Tweet impressions that day alone, talking to so many people who would get screwed out of PPP. What was great about it was that as of noon on April 3rd, a few hours after PPP loan applications were opened, Bank of America was under heavy pressure to amend their guidelines for getting a loan through them. They finally relented, relaxing the rules.

I take partial credit for helping that happen, as I coordinated so many people to retweet each other and discuss as a group on social media how they were getting hosed by their longtime bank for basically not being oversold before COVID-19.

That was a great feeling, and my time helping people with PPP. Over several months, I single-handedly consulted with dozens of small businesses on how to force Bank of America and Wells Fargo to help them complete PPP loan applications and funding of said loans.

Whether it was Mel, a rental designer in Portland with a business called "White Spider," or Bunny and Pirates, an excellent establishment in Florida, I walked them through the landmines that BofA puts in front of people it doesn't want to help. I got them their PPP Loan money. Anything is possible if you are devoted and dedicated to getting it done.

I proved with Mel, Elizabeth, and the countless other people I helped when they were at their lowest point that if you go into a gun battle with a knife, you will lose. You must push back, show you aren't going anywhere, and are not afraid to be in it for the long haul, and maybe you will get helped. If you don't they will run all over you.

The people I helped who were getting railroaded by horrible fucking customer service at Bank of America are the people that makes this country great. If I went on some epic cross-country trip, I could drive by the businesses that I helped, and I can say, "Yep, I am the reason that they are still here after all this."

The banks didn't want to give these people help. They wanted to give people they drooled over help. The Los Angeles Lakers, winners of 17 NBA titles, took out a PPP Loan, as did Shake Shack and Ruth's Chris Steakhouse. Do you think for one fucking fleeting second, anyone within those organizations had to eat a ketchup sandwich for dinner last night because mom doesn't get paid until tomorrow? Do you think they slept in a bed, and a cockroach did a suicide dive from the ceiling onto their face, waking them up? (That happened to me as a kid in my public housing days)

No, of course not. Some small business owners barely get by because they give everything to believe in a dream they had, and meanwhile, their banks were giving out loans to a team that pays Lebron James $35,000,000 a year. It seems a little unfair, right?

There's no doubt that 2020 was the most fulfilling year in my life because I got to have real-life discussions every day about money, finance, and banking. Things are still fucked up for some. That is why I gave my all last year. When I wasn't trying to save small businesses, I was trying to help people deal with their unemployment snafus.

The only difference was that I wasn't trying to help people apply for benefits. No, my work focused on coordinating conversations that customers who were scammed and not helped had with the banks that handled the payment part of unemployment.

Millions of people have waited longer than me to get unemployment in states like California, and some are still waiting for a resolution that they will likely not get any time soon. Reporter Lauren Hepler and CalMatters did extensive reporting on this thing I was a secondary part of by talking with them about my opinions on it. I recommend googling their stuff.

Before I discuss it further, I have to reiterate that big banks in some states handle debit card processing and fraud claims on those debit cards. They aren't taking applications or handling people's job search requirements. That fell on the respective states.

Unequivocally, I can say the State of California has the worst problems with unemployment, and it's not even close. My god, I should be considered a resident of California with all the conversations I had about them.

In a year, I did approximately three interviews for magazines/newspapers, multiple off-the-record conversations with reporters on where to dig up dirt on what's going on. I have had a couple of in-depth discussions for future books on how Bank of America and California had fraud that reached billions of dollars in that state alone. I did a 50 minute Youtube video about my theories about why so much fraud was happening, and my conclusions were simple.

I firmly believe there was a combination of internal fraud or knowledge that Bank of America skimped on preventing fraud, denying claims for legitimate fraud, and strategically closed down banking centers in areas with higher than average unemployment rates.

I knew about Bank of America unemployment debit cards that the cards, with a picture of a mountain on them, were more than likely in sequence. Let me explain.

When we would issue temporary debit cards at the branch, they would come in packs of 100, and all of the cards would be almost the same card numbers, with one or two variations, usually by 3 or 13. Example: 4000 0000 0000 0001, 4000 0000 0000 0004, 4000 0000 0000 0017, and so on. I believe that a lot of cards mailed out to customers were wiped clean before they got to their destination. Unlike my State of New Mexico debit card that was never loaded, these cards were used with the real card never being touched.

While many people try to blame the lack of chips on the card for the fraud, which doesn't hold water to me, many blame Bank of America for not having effectively protected these cards. What did Bank of America do to help prevent fraud after that? Did it refund clients for money stolen? No, it froze the cards of 350,000 people for an indefinite period, citing fraud. Basically, these people were not allowed to use their money until Bank of America determined that their fraud claim was valid, basically thumbing their nose at the normal fraud claim process.

Now, this righteously pissed me off because it accused people who didn't get defrauded of committing fraud or have the potential of being cheated without giving them access to the money they have requested for months. It was causing people to live out on the streets of California. I was in regular contact with a girl in San Francisco sleeping in her car because she couldn't afford half of the rent for an apartment she stayed in with friends. Her name wasn't on the lease, so she was kicked out.

So, what am I complaining about here? This isn't New Mexico, the state who screwed me over many times. I know that, but I am giving you the biggest example I was more than aware of. The state of California contracted Bank of America to handle the fraud claims. That was a fucking disaster.

This is the reason why. I am sure you have heard the phrase "Zero Liability Guarantee" with banks before, right? So what it boils down to is that if they find that you had nothing to do with the fraud, you will get your money back every time.

Sounds good.

Except when you harken back to that adage I am sure some older man in your life said at one time or the other.

"You know who pays for shoplifting? We do because stores have to raise prices because of that."

While I am sure that someone stealing one DVD at Walmart caused dill pickles to go up is something that person believes, it's not the case. Maybe at a tiny mom-and-pop store, yes, but Bank of America is not a mom-and-pop operation.

Bank of America taught me about "performance losses" and "policy losses" when I was a teller and a banker. It is not the PERFECT analogy here, but it'll make things easier to understand what's happening with California Unemployment.

When you work at a bank, a performance loss is when you did something, whether intentionally or not, to cause the bank to lose money. The consumer equivalent of that would be leaving your card out where someone can steal it or telling your adult son he can use it for gas and then he used it for porn. You can't claim fraud when you set a precedent of that person using it in an unauthorized manner.

Policy losses were explained to me that all things being equal, 100 times out of 100 if you did everything the way you should protect yourself from a loss, or someone else was handling that situation, and they did everything they could to prevent the loss, the loss was going to happen anyway, and no one was at fault. The consumer equivalent would be a consistent pattern of use which makes it easy for banks to identify fraudulent activity like a person who only uses their card at Target and Walmart having their card used at ULTA.

Policy losses are losses the bank eats, even when everyone was on the up and up on both sides. It's part of your "guarantee" never to lose money with fraud, but in order for it to work for you, the client, the bank has to see it that way. This didn't happen in California.

Performance losses in a bank pretty much meant you take the burden on that loss. You don't pay out of your pocket to the bank as a worker when you cash a bad check or something. You just lose your job. The consumer equivalent is the bank telling you that they deny your claim because your carelessness caused it.

Policy losses are losses that the bank "owns" for lack of a better term. No one is at fault. They eat the cost and consider it part of doing business. The consumer equivalent of that is them agreeing that it couldn't possibly be you because of location, amount, type of purchase, and other things like that. Your story checks out, because usually banks see these patterns of fraud and know that more than likely, it wasn't you.

So what Bank of America did to 350,000 cardholders and thousands more who had their unemployment money stolen by criminals through no fault of their own? Not a damn thing. They did so much nothing, it stunned me, and I have seen the lowest of the lows with BofA.

Here's the thing that people don't get. Bank of America and, in turn, the State of California said they weren't sure where the fraud was coming from, so they decided the best way to combat it was to keep people from their money. The silly thing from most consumers, who think that just telling their story to the bank accurately will get them help (This is what I stupidly thought too with my unemployment), is that everything would be fixed. I would see people on Twitter complain to the State of California and Bank of America about the fraud and say something like, "You just lost a customer."

But what people don't get is that not only does Bank of America think you ARE NOT a customer, you are just a holder of plastic that Bank of America issued out on behalf of the state. You are not a deposit account-holding customer. These are distinctions that are in the PRO Policy guide at BofA of what defines a "primary" customer. That is not one of them.

Also, do you think at the moment that they would want you? Hell, no... You are unemployed! You have no money, and you won't have money any time soon from the looks of it. You won't be buying a house, bringing $200k to invest, or opening up

CDs. You will be living paycheck to paycheck.

So, "losing you" isn't a big deal to them. They never had you, nor did they want you. You can argue with the state as well, but what are you going to say?

"I'm not going to do business with the State of California again. I've been a resident here for 40 years. You should consider me a loyal Californian."

See how stupid that sounds?

I'm pissed at the State of New Mexico for not approving my benefits and have put me on a fast track for failure whether I work hard or not. What do they have to lose? Nothing. I will still have to pay taxes, be a part of the community, put a sticker on my license plate every year. It's of no risk for them to be dickheads with unemployment because if they aren't helpful, you don't have many options. You are supposedly stuck with a decision, and somehow they can sleep at night knowing that you are FUCKED.

California was issuing unemployment benefits to prisoners, including noted murderer Scott Peterson without any cross-referencing records last year. Did he apply for benefits? No, someone who had access to public files with private information likely did it as a gag. It still showed horrible flaws in the system of how easy it was to scam California unemployment.

But when you open the doors of Walmart, you run the risk of someone running out of the store with some stolen shit every day. Do they close the store to customers? No! So why do you close a much-needed program for months at a time because someone decided to do wrong, and 99.9% waited patiently?

It's because they were overwhelmed. They won't admit it, but people were not ready for the shit storm that came with millions of people begging for money. Walmart was overwhelmed too and is overwhelmed on a typical busy day. They have to keep the doors open, though.

While I am fair in saying that they had no way of knowing the magnitude of what they were expecting, we don't stop caring and trying to help people when it gets hard. Do police officers and firefighters quit when the going gets tough? Do builders quit building something when they come upon an issue that they couldn't foresee? Of course not.

States and banks did.

State unemployment systems were the same all across the country. Here's the thing, though: If they were all consistently horrible, that doesn't justify it as an excuse. A lot of my work helping others this summer mimicked the same shit I have gone through myself during my unemployment process.

Long wait times on the phone, horrible reps on the other end that were contracted employees of a third-party company and not employees of the state or the banks. That's a recipe for disaster. Why? Because when someone from Baca Call Centers LLC (Hey, that is a good business idea for me) answers my phone on behalf of State of New Mexico Unemployment, they only have one boss to respond to. No, not the state. That's just the "company" the call center they work for does business with. They have to answer to their boss on the call center floor or the manager in charge of the WFH people.

That manager cares about call time, the volume of your voice, the number of calls taken, etc. They don't care that Mr. Baca in Southern NM didn't get his unemployment. Hell, they likely don't even know everything about how our state works because that call center might be thousands of miles away.

People I talked to while in banking told me all about the call center life. The person I replaced as sales manager at BofA? She and her hubby met in a call center environment, and her hubby was the head honcho of the local call center, which had a contract with DirecTV. My wife worked for that same call center during the summers while she was in school. She was a bank associate for Citizens Bank in Pennsylvania while she was living in New Mexico!

I had one fantastic experience on the phone, and two other subpar ones, which led me to the stress I have about my money now, and frankly, in retrospect, I shouldn't sugarcoat how fantastic Barry was because he may not have worked for the state. He might have been some slacker dude who gets to work from home and knows he has no pressure in this job, even though everyone on the other end did. Barry was fantastic because he likely had no accountability. He filled out my forms, which inevitably got denied, but he was oh, so lovely, wasn't he?

I genuinely believe some people out there for the NM Department of Workforce Solutions care about helping people. I don't want to say, "Care about their job," because that's different. That implies you will do anything in your power NOT to lose your job. Caring about helping people isn't defined by a linear roadmap that spells it out like, if this person has x and y, he should get z money.

Bank training told me that every person's situation isn't unique, so our "solutions" can easily be tied to their needs. Because my issue had to do with unemployment that COVID-19 triggered, and I was a gig-worker/self-employed, I fell into a different bucket than a bartender at a nightclub or a blackjack dealer at a casino. I was unique.

Consistent service means you treat every person with the same energy, effort, and confidence. Consistent service doesn't mean you give the same advice no matter how different each person's story is. That is where states failed with this, and that is where banks failed.

I'll end this chapter on this note. Do you know how I know unemployment benefit recipients are treated differently by banks? Because I was guilty of mistreating them too. I was part of a Bank of America scheme to make their patronage of my bank horrible.

When I was still a young teller, the State of New Mexico had Bank of America as a fiscal agent for their banking, child support department, and, yes, unemployment. This was right about 2008-2009. I remember it vividly as it was my first year here in Las Cruces. I was immersing myself in everything I could at work to help me advance faster. I asked a million questions of my manager during this time.

Of course, in 2009, unemployment had a slight jump in

the number of people filing for benefits. The economic unrest America had hit New Mexico hard. We had a meeting in our bank. It was about our customer service satisfaction scores, and they were in the toilet. We were the last-rated bank in our region. We were only 1 of 2 New Mexico banks in our El Paso region. Every other Bank of America in New Mexico was in a separate region. We were way behind the leaders in customer satisfaction.

The thing was in a place like BofA when people got surveys in 2009, they weren't surveys you can do on your smartphone. We didn't have smartphones as we do now. They got an old-fashioned phone call right in the middle of fucking dinner. My friend did surveys for some company for a while as a second job, and he told me he got a 95% hang-up rate on people he called. The 5% that stay on the line? Most have a bone to pick with you.

We were graded on a scale of 1-10, and any score eight or lower was rounded down to a 1, which meant our score went down dramatically and impacted sales bonuses and our performance grade. I wasn't getting those bonuses yet at BofA, but I sure heard about it from people eligible to hit those incentives.

The transcripts of the calls from an outfit called Moritz Research had a common theme. Wait time, with an emphasis on the teller line and the speed of tellers.
"I hate going into your bank on Mondays because it's a ridiculous hour-long wait."

So, why Mondays? That was when the State of New Mexico unemployment hit for pretty much everyone who certified their benefits a couple of days beforehand. Those people were told in materials and on the state website that they could withdraw their money at any Bank of America branch. While technically correct, they didn't have to wait at our bank to do the transaction. They could have easily gone to their bank, as the debit card was a Visa and works everywhere. It was merely a suggestion.

But hundreds of people every Monday would blitz our bank, making us always run out of money and keeping that line 10-20 deep. Who gets the surveys? Not the unemployed people, because they aren't "Real" account holders with us, so we didn't have their info to call on them for a survey. My manager said, "They hold a card with our bank's logo on it. We can't let these scores go down more." Disciplinary action for all of us was on the table if we couldn't get this right.

I was booed like a heel wrestler when I would go to work at 9:15 am Mondays. This was when our manager would stagger our shifts. Customers were mad because they assumed I was late or didn't give a shit.

So, who were the people who took the surveys? Mostly cranky older people with money. My manager said, matter-of-factly, these unemployed people have no money, nor do they want an account with us, so we will make THEM wait. They then CHOOSE to remain here if they want their money.

So, the following Monday, we do something drastic. I can't believe I am finally talking about this, by the way. My manager has the idea to put me on a far-away window and says I will be the "unemployment teller." We were going to come up to the clients and greet and intercept them as they walked in. If they needed to access their unemployment money, she would direct them to my line, which was 15x longer than the main line for clients.

She claimed I was the fastest teller, which is why she put me there because I would be able to help more people in less time. I bought into it right off the bat, until the first ass-chewing from those unemployed people, who were bitter and upset, and now they must deal with only me to get their money.

The other customers loved how fast they were in and out. Still, those grumpy unemployed people tore into me every Monday for the next year until Wells took over for the fiscal agent responsibility in 2010. It was a double-edged sword. I got praised for my speed by my boss but chastised by the clients who wanted to get their unemployment money out. Our customer service satisfaction scores went up, giving every teller an "exceed" review every quarter, except me. I got a "meets expectation." Why didn't I get a better performance review?

Because every Monday, I would help over 150 people, many of them the same people every week. I would do my required spiel, offering them the ability to have a checking account with us to put their unemployment direct deposit here at BofA. I would get laughed at often.

"Do you think I would fucking bank at a place that makes me wait an hour to get my money? Fuck no. Give me my fucking money so I can go, please!" was one comment I heard.

So those Mondays were kick-ass for efficiency but horrible for one metric for my performance, my referrals for accounts for those clients. Because I had pretty much all clients say no to me, it brought down my referral sell-through average to where the corporate office was on my boss about writing me up for not selling more proficiently.

Never mind that fucking management thought it was a swell idea to segregate poor people from rich people, aka, unemployed people with no ties to our actual clients and us, creating an atmosphere of classism in our location.

I get chewed out by people every Monday. What can you do with it but KNOW that you did exactly what they told you to do, and you got yelled at still? Meanwhile, because of your efficiency in that segregated teller line, the scores went up, and everyone got rich and a good review....except you.

What a mind-fuck, right?

My former company, Bank of America, treated the clients who received unemployment like second-class citizens until the state up and left us and went to Wells Fargo, which still has them until 2022, according to a PDF on the state website. That agreement is 309 damn pages. This book won't even be that in terms of length. Ha.

Hey, I wonder if they segregate their lines by rich and poor too?

To put it bluntly, the entities that are awarded the duty of helping people who need help are often the ones that don't give a fuck about who is on the other end of the line. It's sad to think, but we are a society of analytics now. Someone will tell you that while all customer service has gone to shit, revenues are up for this reason. Ignore those people. Get down and dirty and help people in need.

Author's Note:

I do want to note that while my time working in banking was miserable, and I disliked my boss for putting me in no-win positions during this time, I understand now, after being a manager myself, how miserable she was treated. I have a million and one horrible things to say about Bank of America and how they are toxic to the customers it services, but in retrospect, I had three really strong female branch managers who taught me a lot.

While I can dislike all of them at times, I know they were also under stress from corporate. My experiences with unemployment a dozen years ago only make sense to me now that I am on the other side of things. It's amazing how people in power regard few people who have these benefits.

But trust me, I have a big fat tasty book about my time at Bank of America almost completed. Stay tuned!

MY STATE: NOT WINNING

Earlier, I dedicated a whole chapter explaining my case to the skeptic who may read this and think I am just a miserable slob who wants free money. This chapter is different because I am not trying to win people over. I am trying to win myself over. Aside from my consumer advocacy project, I try to keep a low profile. I only seek the spotlight if it means that I can help other people with that spotlight.

New Mexico is a fascinating place to live. There is no place like it. While I can opine about the amazing food and the uniqueness of desert life, people have an indescribable romance with the state. Hell, that's why my bank was overrun with Canadians and from cold-weather spots in the United States. There's something about it. Aside from one fleeting moment a decade ago when I contemplated a transfer to Tucson, Arizona, at BofA, I never thought I would leave.

But New Mexico at times revels in mediocrity. We celebrate ignorance. We mostly strive just to get by and don't strive to make a difference. I was guilty of it before I saw that people needed help. I have no million-dollar nest egg to carry me into retirement in thirty years. I am trying to figure out today, much like a vast majority of New Mexicans.

I had some pretty excellent teachers in my time in Socorro, NM, where I graduated high school twenty years ago this year. I know there are still some fantastic teachers. So why the FUCK is my hometown of Socorro, NM, saddled with a 63% high school graduation rate? 63!!!! This isn't dropping out of school to help ma and pa on the farm a hundred years ago. We are in an age where knowledge and education are celebrated and pretty much required to function in other parts of the country. It's not a lie. This information is as plentiful as the crops on ma and pa's farm with all their dropout kids helping. This is a fucking disgrace.

I used to joke with my mom that she would likely be in prison if I went to school today because of how truant I was back in the day. Now, I question that. I feel that James Baca would have slipped through the cracks, and speaking of crack, I would likely be smoking it as well. I think that whoever is supposed to help these kids is just doing enough to get by—what a disgrace.

We have a rampant heroin problem in our state. Rio Arriba County in Northern New Mexico used to hold the distinction of "Heroin Overdose Capital of the World" a decade or so ago. Now, heroin addiction and deaths are at an insane rate everywhere in New Mexico.

I have a sister who battles addiction and has been incarcerated as a result as well. I see from her trials and tribulations of trying to work at a low-end food service job while juggling probation and other things that come with re-establishing yourself as a productive citizen.

She has struggled at times and relapsed. She was in jail for a couple of months earlier this year. My sister has two kids that my 60-year old mom is raising as a result. We pretend to celebrate people who go above and beyond like, but we rarely reward them with anything other than fake kudos on social media.

Recently my sister has shown marked improvement with getting out of that rut. I am proud of her. We don't speak as much as we used to, but we were so close when she was a kid. I root for her because there is no one else who will root for her if not.

A system that claims to want to rehabilitate people in the throes of addiction will also have a person in charge of her probation along with others swing his dick around when he wants to feel that feeling like he's the god of all recovering junkies. Most recently, he denied her permission to leave the county for the funeral for our 3-year-old niece.

Addiction is just as much mental and psychological as anything else. How do you survive a mental ass-kicking like that from a man with a power trip? As long as no one knows about it, he'll get away with it, right? Who'll listen to her complaint? She's a junkie, right?

That's the thing with my state. I keep track of all the recidivism in my hometown daily. I wake up, get a cup of coffee, and whip out the Mobile Patrol App to see who got arrested in my hometown of 8000 people that night. Some people have been arrested 20 times this year (It's October as I write this), and they can legitimately get to 25 arrests. Our New Mexican culture would label me a *mitotero*, a snoop who gossips about others. No, I fucking cry that there are people my age with a shock of white hair and no teeth. They look 60 years old, and they are in their 30s. It's a fucking disgrace.

Why are they continuously getting arrested instead of getting help? Where are the resources to get people out of this rut? Why does everyone complain about the issue, but very few do anything to amplify the problem to give it some attention? Because we are trained in our culture not to get involved. We are selfish. We are self-important. It's someone else's business. It's not your business.

But what do we end up with by not saying something?

We have a police officer that was a subject of an investigation for posting videos that mocked Native Americans that he was arrested on TikTok. These videos contained dangerous racial tropes, including saying that the passed-out Navajos he was arresting were "probably drinking mouthwash." What do we do with news like that? Not much. He still works as a cop and is still arresting those people I mentioned, likely mocking them on TikTok still.

When the local news posted the story, we got a fuckton of people commenting on the story and social media that he deserved a second chance. Again, we revel in mediocrity. The people who were the most outspoken on social media about these things (myself included) were threatened with an ass-kicking. Don't you want your police to be on the news for saving a basketful of kittens stuck in a tree or using the easiest racist joke about Natives on a social media platform where he had thousands of precocious young people thinking it's ok?

I've dealt with this apathy of people in power myself lately. I was the subject of harassing phone calls, messages, and emails from an employee of the city of Socorro for the last two years. It was an old bully that continued to harass me into our late 30s. The messages are coming while he is on the clock at his job, which is equally frustrating. I filed a couple of police reports during that time to get it on the record, and I finally reached out to his boss on the matter.

Since this harasser holds a high-managerial non-elected position with the city, I thought I would get an audience with someone. I didn't. His superior chose to bathe in mediocrity here. He decided my claims were unfounded, and the bullying continues to this day. We choose not to deal with the things that are seemingly wrong with our state, and instead of fixing them, we ignore them.

While all my examples above are personal views and experiences, I can safely tell you that most people feel this way and have similar experiences. The difference between me and so many others? They are told by the culture we grew up in that "Snitches get Stitches." While this is a byproduct of some parents telling their kids that no one likes a tattletale, it has become an inherent part of our culture. We don't want to talk about these things out loud.

While this book is about my experience navigating through the unemployment system, it is more an indictment of a system that has no accountability when something is wrong and is chock full of high-fives when there is any small thing to celebrate.

Aside from a complaint here and there about people getting screwed, you only get stories about how the state is going after people who they claimed defrauded the system instead of figuring out why it happened first. There are even lawsuits filed by some people who feel the way I do that they were denied benefits that they otherwise had qualified for before or were told misleading information as to make them not eligible.

Lawsuits cost money. I don't have money, so I would rather shame them and make money with this book. Seems fair, right? I mean, I AM not clogging up the legal system that so desperately needs legal-strength Rid-X at the moment. Hopefully, there are some readers of this book that have septic tanks that got that small joke. Anyway, I digress.

I understand the need to prosecute to the fullest extent people who illegally take advantage of the system, but do we not believe our state can walk and chew gum simultaneously? Do we not believe that it is possible to multitask here? It just seems like when the spotlight shined away from these benefits, their give-a-shit-bone in their body left as well. That radio silence is an eerie feeling when it is happening to you. 13 years in banking told me that those feelings are real when you think someone is ignoring you and your issue on purpose. It's not fun and is infuriating when you are trying to help someone in front of you, and your supposed "Teammates" choose not to be as helpful.

How can people sleep at night knowing that someone asked for their help, and you refused to give it? How can people function knowing that they hold power to improve the world but choose not to? It's something that I think about every day that I help someone who is losing their dream home because of the bank, someone who got defrauded, and all their bank does is blame them for it happening, and I think about it every day when I wake up to no direct deposit alert of my money.

We spend so much time lauding our oil revenues here, and I can tell you that I know five households that don't currently have indoor plumbing. We talk about how we love the food of our great state, but we don't talk about those restaurants that pay undocumented workers below the minimum wage under the table at some restaurants in this state? It happens in almost every city in New Mexico. My aunt's restaurant was even guilty of it thirty years ago. Instead of shaming the perpetrators, what do people say? Get those fucking illegals out of here!

We shame the victims of exploitation and blame them for all the ills of the world, and the people who violated many laws get a lawyer, pay some fines and continue to be a scourge with a business license.

I'm a member of a restaurant review page in my hometown of Socorro, NM, on Facebook. Like clockwork, every three months, a particular prominent restaurant will post something to the effect of "We are hiring all positions. We are shortening the hours to 4-8 pm, four days a week, due to a lack of staff." Every time, Facebook lights up.

"That damn Biden keeps paying people not to work."

"No one wants to work. COVID-19 made people lazy."

While that second one may be true for some people, I can tell you that this restaurant has posted this APB for jobs about ten times this year, and skipping COVID-19-riddled 2020, maybe about ten times in 2019. There's a virus impacting job performance, and it ain't COVID-19. It's a virus called a toxic work environment. Maybe COVID-19 did give people the epiphany that they don't want to work for assholes anymore but trust me, these business owners have single-handedly run off every able-bodied member of their kitchen staff for a generation.

I distinctly remember a girl named Nicole. She was the sister of a girl I wanted to date in 2005. I recall her being run off from that restaurant for the dastardly deed of requesting Wednesday afternoons off because she was going to be in charge of a youth church group. That was a bridge too far for them, and they let her go, citing her inability to be available on certain days.

This was the most upbeat Grand Canyon University/Dutch Bros Coffee-level perky, happy person, and they made her bitter as hell when that happened. But it was all Biden's fault and the fault of people who don't want to work, right?

People are cruel with their inability to have any empathy for others. If that happened in 2020-21, and she applied for unemployment, I am sure that the restaurant would do anything and everything they can to fight her claim for money, all while bitching and complaining about the lack of people who wanted to work.

I am raring to work hard to build my small business and make sure that I can provide for my household at the drop of a hat. This does not absolve the state of New Mexico from ignoring my claim the way they have this whole year. I mentioned on my Twitter that I was writing this book, and this Albuquerquean, out of nowhere, who doesn't follow my Twitter account, replied to me with this interesting tweet.

"I got denied too. I filed an appeal. I had a hearing. They said they had to create a "ticket" for my payment & I'm still waiting. They say there is no time limit. They have NO accountability. Why aren't they going into work like I am? Pathetic. Sorry for your troubles, man. I look forward to your book."

So that's what I got to look forward to? My appeal can be the most successful one ever, and if I get my denial reversed, they have to create some magical ticket to pay me that has no time limit as to when I can get paid? Doesn't that reek of banking? Doesn't that reek of political speech? I thought we were all in this together, New Mexico?

The reason shit like that happens is because there is no oversight.

This reminds me of the appeal process for suspensions in the NFL. If you are suspended in the NFL, whether for drugs, fighting, or anything else, you are eligible to appeal. This is per the rules of the NFL and your union. The person who hears your appeal? Roger Goodell, the commissioner, aka, the same asshole who suspended you already.

Is he going to say, "After reviewing all evidence, it turns out I was a little out of bounds in handing you a suspension? It is hereby reduced, and I will reprimand the person, me, who gave you this unjust punishment."

No, he's not.

Is that what I am to expect with my appeal? The same entity that shit on my request for months, not even being able to take my call, is going to uphold the judgment that it's not a valid excuse that they didn't pick up my call? Why would people even go through that?

I've met many people in my time as a banker who take their medicine without fighting back when something terrible goes their way. I've had people get defrauded by phony companies, and they didn't want to file a claim because they felt that the claim officer at the bank would judge them on being stupid to fall for it. Sadly, yes, that person likely would judge the victim, but being passive when evil happens to you only makes the people that are meant to help you passive as well.

Much like I believe with my former company, the state wants to wear you into submission and make you quit fighting back. That's why my thing has taken months, along with other people in my shoes.

Finally, I have one close person in my life who got screwed already by the NM Department of Workforce Solutions, my mother-in-law. Last year, when everyone was laid off because of stay-at-home orders, my mother-in-law was laid off from her job in the county she lives in. It's a government job. Yeah, the county she lives in is small in terms of population, but she still works in a place that interacts with the state of New Mexico. She worked in local government!

She filed a claim because she was laid off. Her offices were shut down. There were no court cases, no paperwork, nothing. She had no income, and she was told to apply for benefits, and she ostensibly was going to get approved with the $600 bonus. So, after filling out the necessary paperwork, she waited and waited and waited.

Cut to a couple of weeks later. She was denied.

Denied? Why?

The reason given was that it "looked like someone with her name and date of birth filed for benefits using a Colorado address," so it was discharged due to that. She promptly appealed because not only did she have proof that she had lived in her hometown for 95% of her life, she was WORKING FOR THE COUNTY GOVERNMENT AT THE TIME OF THE STAY-AT-

HOME ORDERS!!! She had her old boss testify as a witness that she lived in New Mexico and worked for her in the COUNTY GOVERNMENT OFFICE in the state of New Mexico, which she had worked at for many years!!!

This is 100% real life, folks.

She was denied again.

She gave up. I mean, how can you win against that? Maybe someone was committing fraud using her name. It's possible. My younger brother once had to appear at some local jail across the state because some other person with his name and birth year had a warrant out for his arrest. So HE had to drive across the state and fix it for them. My mother-in-law's workplace can easily verify any information with the state as the state interacts with her workplace almost every minute of every day.

But, no, denied.

NM Department of Workforce Solutions, and many other similar entities across the country, as I've witnessed through the eyes of my followers on my social platforms, have done this countless times to people, frustrating them into submission. What's the economic impact of the people who got screwed out of money? Fuck the money. What are the emotional and mental effects and carnage that come from such a frustrating process? It's great. I am one of the rare middle-aged Hispanic heterosexual men who are in touch with his feelings, emotions, and mental health. I tell people what I feel when I feel it because I want no one else to feel like that.

This has made me a wreck when I am used to being a monster truck, breaking down walls to help people in need with bank issues. It's funny because when this happens to someone else, I am guns blazin', will do anything to make sure that person is heard by a system meant to ignore. While this is happening to me, I whimper and cower like a dog because I figured in my heart of hearts, I have my shit together, and they would see that.

But this is a state that loves to thrive in mediocrity, and I see that right now first-hand.

GIVING BACK - MY MISSION GOING FORWARD

About a month ago, I went to Casa De Peregrinos, a local food bank here in Las Cruces, NM, to donate a bunch of food I accumulated. No, I didn't get it through food stamps, nor did I steal it. I am an extreme couponer. With that, I have found strategies in couponing that keep my food budget extremely low, which has helped me a lot. It also has allowed me to have excessive amounts of food.

Navigating through the driveway into the back donation center is one part overwhelming and another part heartbreaking. You would have thought that you were in the Sam's Club parking lot on a Saturday. That's how busy it was there. Car after car was loaded up with food for free, which was generously donated by people, workplaces, and grocery stores. It's food that can allow people to eat for a couple of weeks at a minimum, and it's all gratis. But when you see 20-30 parking spaces continuously full loading up groceries for people who can't afford it and can't get benefits from the state in some cases, it makes you cry.

So I head to the back of the building, as I have done a few times before, and I try to flag down someone with a dolly. All of them are so busy unloading trucks, and I am there with my meager donation. I was feeling bad I didn't have more to give. The breakneck pace they get shit done is impressive to me, and I am in AWE of the people there, many of them volunteers.

I finally locked eyes with a man about 15-20 years older than me. I told him that I had some food to donate and if someone could help me unload it. He pointed at a shopping cart, and I told him, "No, it's much bigger than that." I then point him in the direction of my Jeep Liberty, and he sees three big boxes in the back, and he goes to get a luggage cart.

He meets me at my trunk, and he points to the boxes like, "Man, this is a teamwork job. You are a big dude. Help unload this shit." He didn't say that, but I saw it in his eyes. I am a dude who fancies himself a gym rat, and at one time, I was powerlifting quite an amount of weight. These boxes were...well, boxy and oblong. Not heavy, just cumbersome. I lifted them and placed them on the cart.

The guy then looks at my 40-50 boxes of cereal, 100 jars of peanut butter, and all the rest of the stuff, and he very earnestly says words that blew my mind.

"This stuff isn't expired, is it?"

I come back immediately with an "of course not," and I chuckle underneath my facemask. It was too quick at the moment to find that question offensive, and all I could do was muster a nervous laugh because it was a question I was not expecting. I wait around for a few minutes so I can get a receipt of my donation. It's not necessarily for my taxes or anything, but mainly proof that I give back despite the hurdles my project and my fight with the state have put me in.

While I wait, I look at the line of people waiting to get into the building to get food. It rivals a Black Friday event at a department store or concert ticket sale to Garth Brooks or Metallica. It's pretty stunning, and even more because as I probably stared a little too long at the line, I started recognizing people from my past as a banker.

Hey, that's Mr. You-know-who. Wow, that's Mrs. So-and-so. Holy cow, that's Mr. Such-and-such.

These are people I helped when they were customers at my bank. Because I am blessed and cursed with a photographic memory at times, I vaguely remember how much they would have in their accounts or how much they got paid at their jobs. This was my talent at the branch. I could make any client feel like someone significant to BofA when all I did was take an interest in their financial goals personally.

I was saddened. I don't know what's going on with them now, but I never thought I would see these folks waiting for a handout of food. They weren't rich, but I would put them at a line of "barely getting by" at the very least. This broke my heart because I talked to these people often.

I get my receipt, and I drive off. I roll up my windows on a hot day because, shamefully, I don't want to lock eyes with these people who know me, and I know them. I drive down the road leading to the main drag and see people in sleeping bags sleeping under bushes and trees and some up against the buildings that line the area.

We are in a pretty rough world now, whether we like to admit it or not. Seeing those sights and working in a bank in that neighborhood gave me intimate knowledge of what people go through. The people that I saw there that I didn't think were going through some stuff woke me up further. I was going through a lot of things emotionally on my long ride home.

Do people donate rotten food to the face of people needing help? If so, why? If not, why did he ask me that question? Did I not look trustworthy enough, or was my food horde too big not to question how I got it? It was just a bizarre moment in a moment of generosity.

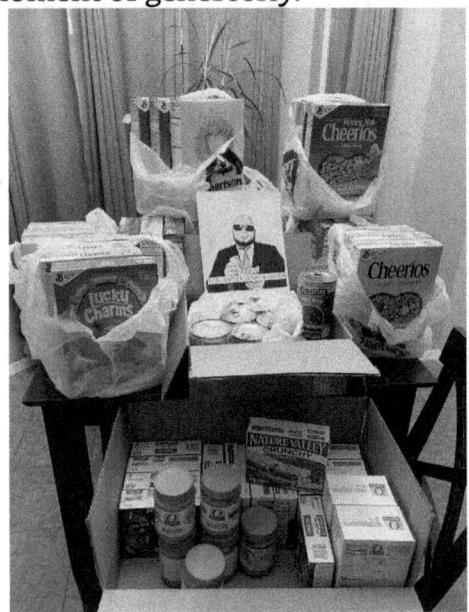

I couldn't get over seeing those former customers in that food line. I wondered if they were going through the same thing I was going through with the New Mexico Department of Workforce Solutions. I wondered if they hit a point where they were so hard up for money that going to a food pantry simply made sense. This pandemic has opened up the eyes of a lot of people who finally see people in need. At the same time, it has quietly made people assholes into thinking that everyone is just looking for a handout without knowing the context as to why they are in dire straits.

A couple of weeks ago, I watched a news story on our local ABC affiliate station in Las Cruces, KVIA, in El Paso. They were reporting on the announcement that the same food pantry was getting nearly $4 Million from our city to purchase a bigger building to expand their operations to help so many more people. The building that I traveled to was getting a little long in the tooth, so I am sure this money was a godsend to those folks.

But of course, like everything else in this world now, on social media and in the council meeting where this was discussed, there were some people who not only were against it, they took the time to rail on how the city has a homeless problem. "Something needs to be done about it," according to them.

How can you be against using money to buy a huge abandoned commercial building to use it to feed people in need?

Because people are ignorant, they see the person begging on the street asking for a buck as the same person who was in one of those cars loading up a trunk full of free groceries. They think that the person on the street is indicative of who food pantries are exclusively providing to during the pandemic.

Ok, yes, some of those folks on the street are also being helped, but the people I saw? I knew these people to be gainfully employed people with bills and responsibilities loading up food to eat. The average citizen who doesn't know these people is conflating the problems into one. While home insecurity is bad and rampant in many cities, my New Mexico city included, the vast majority of people seeking food are your neighbors.

According to Casa de Peregrinos, New Mexico is the second-worst state for hunger for our seniors and the third-worst for our kids. This is a real-life issue, and when I am here writing about my fight to get my backpay unemployment approved, I think about these people because I met these people over the years before I had to worry about money. That person bitching about this gift from the city to help others does NOT realize that.

I'm not a man of faith, nor do I believe in Karma, but I do believe that if you have the means to give back, you should go ahead and do it. The half-ton of food I have donated this year came at very little to no cost to me to give because of my couponing prowess. By putting in a little effort, I can sleep at night knowing I have likely helped dozens of people feel full for the first time in a while. I freaking hate tooting my own horn, but it took a long time for me to feel the need to give back, much less do it.

I have donated multiple times this year, and I don't make a big deal about it to anyone. I share with my Twitter followers who support everything I do, and in some cases, contribute as well. During the summer of 2021, as the free-lunch program was fledgling, I was able to donate hundreds of boxes of cereal, and I called it the "Notorious Banker's Summer Breakfast Stimulus." It was so freaking awesome

The Notorious Banker's Summer Breakfast Stimulus

I call myself a survivor, but those people run laps on me. They have to do it regardless of the pandemic or not. They already know the system favors the system and not them. They don't have the voice or the confidence to call out injustice as it is happening to them, and they are stuck deep into a vicious cycle that will spin them around until they are six feet under.

Part of the uniqueness of my consumer advocacy project is that I get to speak to people, both rich and poor, about issues in the banking industry. I helped someone keep an $800,000 home loan alive, and I also helped someone on a fixed income get an overdraft fee back on the same day. One person is not like the other in terms of money, but that day, both came to me via social media and asked for my help because they both felt powerless. Thanks to Dr. V for the trust earlier this year!

I got both of them what they wanted, and I had the fortune of sharing their stories on the same day, as I mentioned on Twitter. Weirdly, I felt like it bridged the gap between people from two worlds who learned that people in power would find a way to flex that power when they want, and if you don't know how to seek help, you will lose against them.

The people at the food pantry had to realize in their heads that they "lost" whatever game of life they were playing, and they decided to ask for help. Most people in this town likely don't know the depth of how much that food pantry helps the citizens of Las Cruces.

So, why do I talk about this food pantry? I have no affiliation with them short of my donations, and I have no intentions of ever working at a place like that. Why? Because I think I would shed tears the second I saw those people I cared for at my old job for so many years. To see them wheel out a cart of day-old bread and near expired dairy because they were likely screwed over by the government in some fashion, maybe my former bank, or worse yet, "Trusted" friends and family would be hard to swallow regularly.

I thought my place in banking was a liaison between people in need and people who can change your fortune at a snap of a finger. I've seen it happen. This is why I dealt with working there for so long.

This chapter is called "giving back" because I am going to make it my mission to help anyone and everyone call attention to their battles. Whether it is with NMDWS, Snap Benefits, Big banks being difficult to deal with during the pandemic, and anyone who negatively impacts someone else, during these "unprecedented times" where we claim to come together.

I will write letters, make phone calls, and send emails

on behalf of people who feel like the system has screwed them. If they don't have the words, I will talk to them to find those words, and I will use my God-given talent in writing and find someone to pay attention to help them out, or at least give them an audience.

Complaining about customer service in the last few years has developed a connotation with a specific "K" name to lampoon angry customers. Not all clients are that "K" word. Some people need help. I will be that liaison to make sure they aren't just passed off as a "K" word, and I will make sure that I would be labeled a homophone of that word...Carin'.

My wife and I talked about how long I could last if I ever decided to re-enter the world of banking. I think my conscience will no longer let me work at a place like that simply because you see how much they negatively impact many clients. I couldn't give back to people knowing that the company I worked for is taking so so so much from them and have a clear mind.

I am a killer at sales. Hopefully, I convinced you well enough to buy this book, and if I did, thank you so much for allowing me to buy a Spicy Chicken Sandwich at Chick-Fil-A today. But would my customer service skills and compassion benefit people if I was a Nissan salesman? No, it would only help the dealership I work for.

I would be whoring out my skills to get people into a 72 or 84-month payment plan for some car they really can't afford. I can't believe 84-month payment plans are a thing, by the way. I wasn't married 84 months ago, and it feels like I have been for 20 years. I can't be the person to lock down someone for almost a decade in a car that they can't afford to take anywhere on a vacation.

One of the biggest knocks of people on the job market now is people who say, "Think you are too good to flip burgers or clean hotel rooms?"

No, I am not too good to do that. I come from a long line of blue-collar workers. My grandfathers as laborers. My mom and dad worked as a manager and chef at a restaurant, respectively. My stepdad shoveled shit at a ranch, and my second stepdad was a cook before he became a construction worker. Don't ever put that on me that I am not willing to get dirty.

However, if you love sports and follow sports closely, you know that a basketball team isn't made up of people who can shoot lights out and handle the basketball up the court. There's only one ball is the cliché people use to point out that you need big guys to set up screens to let the shooter shoot. You need someone with long arms to play killer defense to ensure the other team doesn't beat you. A team isn't just the best group of people. It is the best fit of players with different individual skills that can collectively use those skills to better the team.

Blue-collar work isn't beneath me, but I can be a much better productive member of society by being the mouthpiece for those who need help against so many entities that have wronged them. I think my destiny was to experience this hardship put on by the State of New Mexico to empower me to be more vocal about these things and network with similar people who need help that otherwise have no one to speak for them.

I have an impressive resume from my bank days, yes, but you should see the resume I have now of people I have who can vouch for how hard I worked for them when everything was utterly hopeless, or so it seemed. I made lifelong believers in my skills and my desire to better what is so wrong with the way poor people and people of color are systematically screwed daily.

I always tell people when I talk about banking that it's more than just everyone agreeing that "Overdraft Fees Suck!" You also have to understand that most overdrafts are triggered by suggestions a bank or a business made to you to "simplify your life." It simplified you to the point of no fucking money because whatever checkmark you clicked on to authorize, say, an auto-pay for Netflix, you neglected to read the terms of Netflix and, in turn, the bank. Both of those say, "You are doing this of your own volition, and we are not responsible for any fees incurred by your authorization."

You allow us to get our money either way, and there's

nothing you can do about it. While I am a person who loves technology and banks exclusively online, I can see landmines for so many people who are inattentive to their banking in real-time. That is where I feel I can give back as well. I can show people how to effectively manage their money without letting THEM (meaning the banks and other big entities) win.

I was reading a biography of Jack Whittaker, who was at one time, about 2 decades ago, the biggest Powerball winner in the history of the game. He won $324 million, which ended up being about half that after taxes. Reading through this story, which I remember bits and pieces about from back in the day, was enlightening.

There was a lot of tragedy, drugs, and poor decisions he and his family made after he won the jackpot, but I think there were a lot of life lessons that they gave and learned that we should share.

First off, he was born in the bowels of West Virginia, dirt poor. If you have ever been to some parts of rural West Virginia, you can almost imagine it to be a greener version of an impoverished New Mexican neighborhood. Many people, including the media, didn't pick up on, save for this Washington Post article I read, that he was a self-made multimillionaire when he won the money. He owned a construction company, and at that time of his winning the lottery, he was worth about $17 million.

So get this, some people denigrated him for even winning the lottery for committing the crime of living the American Dream to the point where he became a man with money and power before five white balls and one red ball changed his life.

The grittiest part of the story that even made me cringe? It wasn't until after he won the Powerball money that the extended hands came out. The city he grew up in effectively disowned him for not donating $10,000 to improve some park in that town. People were livid. He also became a cast-off in his stomping grounds as the gas station/restaurant he bought the winning ticket at, along with breakfast every day for years, as it became a place where people stalked him along the aisles begging him for money. Many had claimed that they were sick or had family members that were sick.

It was reported that he spent hundreds of thousands of dollars a year on Private Investigators to vet these people's stories before he handed any money out. Of course, most of the claims were fake, and it just led him to disenchantment, which eventually led to alcoholism, divorce, and a granddaughter, his shining light, passing away to drug abuse. He was tossed aside by the small town who raised him and got him to millionaire status through blue-collar work and spit him out when they asked for his "extra" money that he won.

Where are you going with this, James? Are you implying your story is made up? What are you saying? Calm down, let me take you to what I am getting at.

So, all things being equal, the man paid about $90 million in taxes out of that jackpot in state and federal taxes. West Virginia has a max of 6.5% tax, which is higher than New Mexico as well. Part of being a citizen in good standing is paying your taxes when you have to, and even if the man played with the numbers on his construction business, there's no way to avoid taxes on a lottery windfall, so he had to pay.

That being said, don't you for at least one second agree that his $90 million tax bill is philanthropic enough at that point? Some of that tax money that went to his state, which was not that amount of money, of course, goes into a general fund and then can be allocated to other projects like...the park they wanted to improve.

"So, James, you are siding with a lottery winner over $10,000 bucks that is probably his pocket change?

Yes, I am. Because for the same reason, I am asking for the unemployment money wrongly denied to me. I put into the system with years of hard work, paying taxes, and not abusing the system. I did my part to help others. Now YOU should do YOUR part in helping others in need, state government!

I am merely asking for what was our right during the pandemic. Jack Whittaker felt the same way. He figured, "Hell, they got a huge chunk of my money. Hopefully, they know how to use it correctly."

While the state of New Mexico has been pretty good in some aspects of COVID-19 relief, what I have seen with my own two eyes as it pertains to need tells me they aren't doing enough to help others.

It's unique that I have a story to tell about my trials and tribulations with unemployment, all the while telling you there are others far worse off. Dealing with my crap will hopefully allow me to highlight others who go through the same thing, or at least shine a spotlight on others who have the same issues.

I was going to save this for my book about Bank of America, but I want to mention it here. It's about giving back. When I was at BofA, there were times they were brutal with their scheduling. You can work a 40 hour week, but because of strategic lunches and all these weird breaks they incorporated to give you off when it's slow, you were in the building maybe 52 hours a week. Yet you were only paid 40, of course.

As a banker, I was offered the opportunity to volunteer at various local events over the years. Events to combat cancer, AIDS, domestic violence, and Christmas food drives were some of the things I was asked to be a part of, but I couldn't do it because of "Schedule adherence" at BofA. Schedule adherence kept us in the building, not getting paid on the off chance we were busy and they needed us.

I felt horrible. It was shitty to hold a prominent role as a supervisor/sort of manager at a bank with thousands of clients, some with a lot of good causes they support, and you can do nothing at all to help them. It was weird telling people no when it was going to be for the betterment of a group in need.

Cut to the Summer of 2012. I am sitting in my apartment at 3 pm. I got off early that day from work. I got a call from my boss, and she said she needed me for a photo opportunity. I asked what. She said that Bank of America was giving money to charity, and they needed a photo when presenting the check. She said that we had gotten a check at the bank from BofA's charitable arm, and we were given instructions on who to give it to.

I had remembered signing for a FedEx envelope that morning and giving it to her, so I assumed that's where she got the check from. She told me to meet her at the branch, and we would go in her car to the Women's Shelter in town where we were going to present the check. I said, "Ok." I was told you never challenge your boss ever, and I wasn't here. I got in my car and went to the bank.

When I got into her office, I asked her a little more about this. She said, "You know, I dunno. They just told us to do this. She showed me an email she got from someone talking about the check for $2,500. It was a weird letter. I am going to be paraphrasing what was said on the email because I didn't take a pic of it, nor was it mailed to me, but it was something to the effect of,

"Hey, Diane. We would like you to present this check for $2,500 to the XXXX Women's shelter located at XXXX in Las Cruces, NM. The director's name is XXXX, and she will be called on the morning of XXXX informing her that you will be presenting the check. Take a junior employee with you for a photo op as well, as we look to show that our company commits to empower women, not just inside the bank. Please submit your photo to us for inclusion to BCO (Banking Center Online)."

BCO was their internal website that was BofA propaganda to its employees every day. Before I went with her, I told her how weird of an optic it would be to have me, a humongous, ominous-looking man, at a women's shelter. I don't know. It just didn't feel right. She downplayed my concern, and we headed to the shelter, about a mile away.

I had thrown on my suit to be a part of this thing that didn't exist to us until we opened that FedEx. The way corporate scheduled us, we had no way of networking with these people, so we were going into something very unfamiliar to us and presenting money we didn't know existed to them all within the same day.

We got a secretary to take a photo of me, my manager, and the director of the women's shelter holding the check with my cell phone, which is why I still have the picture. My boss didn't want to give me her phone for some reason to take the photo. When we got back to the bank, she told me to email it to our boss, and I could go back home. I did just that and left for the day.

At the beginning of my shift the next day, I had 100+ emails from associates across the Bank of America network praising my boss and me for our "Extraordinary work helping women in need" and "giving back to our community." They said we were angels on Earth, and we were a pillar of the BofA community. My manager got similar emails as well.

There we were, in the middle of the Bank's intranet site, with 204,000 employees seeing how James and Diane gave back to a women's shelter in their hometown and presented a check to help these women get a fresh start. While I am glad that they got the money, I never felt more like a fucking phony in my entire life. I swear to you, when I would see the profile photos of the people from BofA who emailed me, it was all a specific demographic of women ages 25-65. People that you know would cry at sappy Lifetime movies. This was all choreographed to show that "We (Bank of America) care!"

Seeing the email beforehand and KNOWING that we had never interacted with that non-profit before or after that, and instructions given to us by someone who likely sent 1000 of those out asking the same things of other branches just made me feel wrong. The person who sent us that money to give wasn't local, didn't know our town from any other, and so coldly told us how to spice up the photo to look awesome.

Deep down inside, I resented that fakeness of that moment, and it was one of a few seeds planted about what a weird, toxic place BofA was.

But knowing how great the lengths it took for a

company to be phony in pretending to care and how little I have to work to make a difference in my community, and with so many people experiencing financial hardships, is astounding. I commit to doing more with my community if and when I can have my unemployment funds sent to me. I will do it regardless because it will be genuine, unlike so many states, cities, and big companies are giving back.

My question is, what more can the state do in helping these people in need as well? No photo ops, please, send real-life help to these people with real-life problems.

Thank You. Please donate to your local food bank and women's shelters if you can!

(2012 photo of myself [with hair], my boss, and the head of a women's shelter after my former company Bank of America donated $2,500 to them. The bank ORDERED us to do a photo op despite never meeting these people before or since, as if we were actively helping them prior to this gift.)

"TRAMPOLINE MONEY" - MY DETAILED PLANS FOR MY UNEMPLOYMENT BENEFITS

Before I begin, perhaps I should talk to you about the name of the chapter. I WAS A HATER before I was reflective enough to understand how people who don't have money react when they got a large sum of money. I was someone who took something that was a blessing to others to the lowest common denominator.

Trampoline money refers to a conversation I once had with a fellow bank teller during income tax time. It seemed that every spring, we would have both friends on social media and customers of ours who weren't really well off getting these HUGE tax returns, and a good majority of them purchased trampolines as part of their windfall.

It was a joke born out of truth, as dozens of people in my life ended up with trampolines in spring, only to sell them by summer because they didn't use it, and they needed money after squandering all of their tax return. But just, FYI, in the summertime, check out your local Facebook buy and sell page. You'll see what I mean.

I also have a couple of trampoline recidivists in my life, buying multiple unnecessary trampolines over the years with a tax return instead of paying bills.

I felt like such an asshole mocking people and their spending all these years later, and it's not because I am a poor spender—quite the opposite. I overthink even a $2 cup of coffee at times, breaking down whether I can afford it in the long run or not. That's just the wiser, older, former relationship manager in me now.

Sitting down with those who got those windfalls and seeing them try to do right by opening up savings accounts for kids and paying off bills made me humanize their plight a lot more. People in need try, but often, the stressors of trying to get on track get derailed by something else, and many people choose to wallow in the muck that is their finances after that.

I think the hypocrisy of my final job title at Bank of America, relationship manager, made me humanize a lot of problems that were going on with my clients. I am writing this chapter because I often think of a question I had to ask every person who came into the bank or my office with a large deposit.

"What are your plans for this money?"

The question was half-hearted, though, as no matter the answer they gave, I was supposed to turn it into a conversation about opening up accounts with us. I had the same skill as some frat boy turning the topic to sex with any co-ed in his sight. It's just...gross.

It was part of my job. There were managers with a pen and clipboard listening to me oversell these poor bastards when they didn't need all these accounts because it was my JOB, and I could lose it if I didn't do that. Not every deposit into a bank account has to mean something, but my role was to make more meaning to it than you made.

I think finances are private, and people shouldn't be judged on their piss poor spending unless it impacts family and friends around them, or leads to some legal action, be it criminal or civil. As part of my advocacy project, I help people who have their accounts frozen by big banks due to purchasing crypto, using their cards to gamble legally on sports, or buying cannabis in a state where it's legal. This happens often and causes some to be unable to bank. It's not my business what they use their money on when it's legal. That's why I go to bat for them.

In the interest of full disclosure and the book I am writing, I will share with you some of my plans for the $20,291 I believe is owed to me by the State of New Mexico. No, I am not buying any trampolines. I was just gifted one by my brother last week. No, he didn't buy it with his income tax return. He has a decent job and a little extra money.

Why am I doing this? As a meaningful, honest, earnest way of showing you a couple of things. One, how practical my spending is. Before I swipe a debit card for something I want, I have probably thought of that moment a hundred times before and how it will impact my budget going forward. I have nothing out of the ordinary on my list of things I want to do. Yes, I want to take a mini-vacation from the grind that is the advocacy I do, but I can make it on the cheap. Trust me.

I spent $62 on a 2-day trip to Vegas in August 2021 with my brother to see WWE Summerslam. $25 for a ticket, $25 for gas, and $12 for a meal. I had packed a ton of snacks from home that I got for free couponing. Hotel? I got it for free by playing a slot machine app on my phone. Transportation? I freaking walked everywhere. I am a man who spent $2000 a trip to Vegas in my 20s. I sure as hell know how to be a cheapskate in my 30s. It's simply about cutting back.

Secondly, I want to show you that the things that I will spend money on almost exclusively will benefit me, and frankly, others in the long run. It's a comprehensive plan to better myself as I go into the second act of my life. I think many of the things I have been pining for since December when the $300 extra benefit kicked in are things you wouldn't think that I was thinking about. If I pay the debt, better my health, and help kickstart a business that will help people immensely with their money going forward, you are likely to say, "Why doesn't James have the money right now?"

Thirdly, I want to show that even self-proclaimed "financial specialists" like yours genuinely fall into the trappings of life in America. Student loans, health concerns, and bills are what's on my mind, and I look forward to taking care of a lot of them.
Finally, I want to share with you what these things mean to me emotionally. There is one thing I want to spend some money on that I hope will get you talking about how we treat each other and how we need to make sure we can be our mentally best at all times without interference from other people who wish to harm you.

I expect the laughing emojis on social media about my book. I expect people to take this shit out of context. Hell, I think that's America's most significant export aside from oil and textiles. Taking shit out of context. Nothing more American made than that. I don't care; however, I will be the guy in the paint on the basketball court taking the charge so other people and I can speak out on being screwed out of money promised to them. I'm ready for this discussion.

So, America, some of you may think that fighting for my $20,291 is silly, but let me show you the "creature comforts" I will pay for with this money. There is no spending spree that I will do with this money. All of it is for a purpose to better my life, my family's life, and to be able to provide a service to the community I love. I don't like sharing my personal business usually, but I feel it neccesary here. Here Goes:

Medical Care

I am guilty of one thing in my thirties. That is neglecting my health. What do they say about people in their 20s? Something something something invincible...or something like that. I felt that way. I was a chubby teen, a chubby early adult, and then I decided to reinvent myself by losing a lot of weight.

Age 20: 285lbs
Age 21: 195lbs

Losing weight was my proudest achievement at that time. After that, I was a gym rat, going nearly every day. I ate pretty decently, and I prided myself on being able to wear nice clothes, especially when I got into banking. As time went on and my career enveloped my brain, focus, and energy, I started losing the battle in my mid-30s.

Hair loss is minor compared to all the other shit you go through. Because of the stress involved in my career, I would have these unexplained headaches that would persist throughout the day. It seemed like every curveball thrown in my day by my job would lead to these stress headaches.

I used to think people were full of shit when they mentioned things like that. The masculinity that I had would deem that person soft and ill-equipped to handle a tough job. Now I know everything is interconnected. I never got that way in any other situation other than banking.

I would sleep for hours out of mental exhaustion right after work, impacting dinner and the rest of the day with my wife. I would go to the gym late at night to work out my frustrations, but I would always get reset to zero when I went into the bank. It sucked the life force out of me, and this is how I found out it was the job.

I got fired, and it felt like I was released from prison mentally. I felt so free and loose and happy again. Aside from this stretch fighting with the state about money (See how money affects everything?), I was pleased with the new path I charted in life. But the damage was done.

One of the things Bank of America prides itself on is its "amazing" benefits package for employees. Yeah, two weeks paid vacation is pretty sweet for branch employees, and you get more as you last longer there, but they tout tuition reimbursement, and of course, a fantastic healthcare plan. For a lot of my ex-coworkers who used their healthcare a lot for their kids, they would tell you it is pretty decent. I have no reason to doubt them. But the shit those co-workers used to get influenced my financial decisions as well. Why?

Because in my 20s, I decided I didn't need health insurance because I was invincible, remember? But in my 30s, as these small things crept into my life, I knew I wasn't invincible. I was avoiding more stress and anger by not getting health insurance.

Huh?

Let me explain. I didn't do health insurance, but I did get a vision plan because my eyes are jacked. I have been pretty blind since high school. I think 20/80 is where I was last time in both eyes. I was in front of a computer 16 hours a day for work and play, and I knew my eyes were something I needed to be proactive on because they were something I beat to death every day.

You are supposed to put every time-off request in some magical calendar two months in advance at BofA. The rule of most branches is that two people can't be off simultaneously, regardless of whether they have different jobs or responsibilities, which is stupid. You combine that with long-tenured staffers with 5-6 weeks of vacation, all the other employees' vacation requests, and black-out dates (first week of every month and every holiday week), and you have no time, nor any chance to do anything.

I got the vision plan in 2013, and I tried calling in for an appointment two months in advance, and every doctor on the vision plan I had didn't schedule that far out for new clients. Plus, the doctors on the plan were not around on weekends as well. They were all old-timers with offices that looked just as old as they did. I told my regional manager at the time that I needed to have an exception, and she was livid.

"Ugh, James. It seems like you JUST don't care about the team. It's all about you. I have to question your commitment to Bank of America when I hear you ask for special treatment like that."

It was a fucking eye exam. I was blown away at the comments, but I would come to find out that's par for the course at BofA (You'll see why in the mental health part of this). She made an exception for me to have a morning off to get an appointment done, but I would have to work from 11 am-4:15 pm. I thanked her, and I scheduled an appointment two weeks out at 8 am.

So, I went and got my eyes checked. What I didn't factor in was the fact that my eyes were going to get dilated. When they did that, my eyes were out to lunch AND dinner. I could barely see and leaving the doctor's office straight to the bank. I was thankful I didn't wreck. (For the record, the eye doctor was two blocks away, and I could drive that with my eyes closed anyway).

I toughed it out through a day of work, which is amazing in retrospect. I must've looked like a fool squinting at everything and working slow as can be so I do not make a mistake. But, since my job was sales, I had to account for the branch's new account goal. I didn't have anything. It was not a day to sell accounts. I was pretty impacted by my eyes being dilated.

Bank of America wasn't having any of that shit. All salespeople had to be on a 4 pm conference call and share with their fellow bankers/managers across the region how many accounts they opened and what was originally their goal. When I said my goal was six, and I had 0, I got an ass-chewing from the regional manager on the phone with 60 people listening, saying that performances like that are unacceptable. Other people could do my job for me if I didn't care about the company that much.

My boss totally threw me under the bus too. She chimes in on the call, "I will make sure James is better and ready to go tomorrow." I know they loved that rah-rah shit there, but a simple "You know James came into work barely able to see and worked a computer job for 5 hours when most people would have called in. That's commendable." would have been great.

It was at that moment that I said I would never fucking get insurance again at Bank of America if it meant going through that shit to fix my health. Ever. Why waste money on something that they are going to try not to let you ever use? That was how I felt about it. I never called in sick or asked for time off again. Plus, I haven't been to a doctor in 21 years.

I need to, though.

There are things I need to fix, get looked at, and take care of before it becomes a snowball rolling down a hill. I stupidly took the Obamacare penalty for the last seven years because of the work thing and because I couldn't afford insurance after I left BofA. Co-pays and deductibles for the things I think are needed amount to a lot of money, and this is money I fully intended to pay with my backdated unemployment benefits that NMDWS screwed me out of.

Part of the CARES act was the ability to sign up

for healthcare until the end of 2021 with a subsidy that made the monthly payment, which was $350 a month, free because that is EXACTLY how much my insurance costs. I jumped right on it, knowing that I was going to get my money. Then this bullshit happened, and here I am writing a book. This insurance, which expires at the end of the year, is burning a hole in my pocket. I can't get any of the things done I need to get done. Based on the numbers I am aware of now, I won't be able to afford a comparable healthcare plan in 2022, so I will be uninsured. The state of New Mexico incompetence is causing me to avoid addressing these issues.

Now let's talk about my maladies. First off, my feet. To say that feet are the bane of my existence would be a massive understatement. One of the things that I used to get made fun of as a teenager is now one of the things that cause me the most pain currently. I have flat feet. I mean FLAT. It hurts to stand. It hurts to walk. It hurts to put a lot of pressure on them.

One of the weird unexplained things of the last five years is that my feet have grown several sizes from a 12M to a 14EEEE, and even the EEEE shoe is not comfy enough. I wear shoes with very loose or no shoestrings, like the cool kids do now, except I'm old and uncool. I have no fucking clue why my feet grew in my mid-30s, and they are still growing, and it sucks.

Also, something that can be attributed to this pain I have is visibly evident on my feet. I have discoloration on both feet. Dark red/brown spots on my toes up to my ankles. My wife laughs at me when I try to diagnose it on WebMD, but I mean, don't we all do that?

From what I gather, I have some mad circulation issues, especially in my left foot. It makes sense because I also have fatigue, swelling in my legs, and cramps aside from the discoloration. That shit scares me. It's been a seven-year thing now, and I got to look at that asap. I was thinking of insoles for my flat feet and someone to accurately diagnose what I believe is a circulation issue. But what do I know? I'm not a doctor, that's why I wanted to go to one WITH MY MONEY!

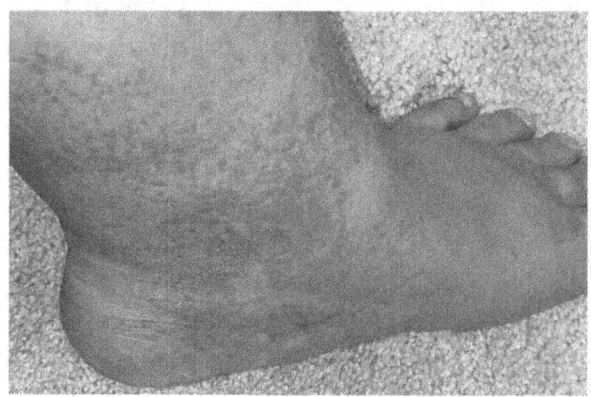

Aside from my Sultenfuss bear claw (dated movie reference), I have a weird irregular mole on my side. It popped up last summer, and while it has gotten bigger, it's still relatively small. Though as I write this, within the last week, Rachel Maddow, noted TV host, announced she had a mole removed that was skin cancer. Although she is "fine," it is still, in fact, cancer. I would love someone to take a look at this, because what do I know? I am not a doctor. That's why I wanted to go to one!

My eyes! I mentioned it earlier. I have terrible eyesight and seven-year-old glasses that no longer work for me. I think LASIK would be a little too pricey but spending a little to get some decent eyeglasses would be great. I used to be one of those people who was too vain for eyeglasses. Screw that. I would love to see.

Maybe this is too personal, but I feel like my testosterone is out of whack. I see all those commercials with old professional athletes suffering from "Low T," and I can relate to the symptoms.

Occasionally, I can feel beastly at the gym, but sometimes yard work can kick my ass. I think part of men's health is men not talking about what makes them feel not as manly as before, and that's embarrassing to them. With my 6'2" 295lbs burly, muscular physique, you never believe I think that way. I am. I definitely would love to see a doctor about how I can overcome this one as well.

My sinuses have kicked my ass for four years now. I notice them inflamed when I do strenuous activities like lifting weights or running around with my nieces and nephews. I also feel tremendous pressure on the top of my nose when I lay on my side, and I feel air releasing like a balloon letting out air.

The air then leaves a bad taste in my mouth, which causes halitosis. It's some sort of post-nasal drip thing, and it sucks. It's so embarrassing.

I am reminded of a conversation I had with my last branch manager in which she mentioned her husband had a sinus infection for fifteen years! (Did he work at a bank too?) He finally got up the courage to go to the doctor, and a week later, it was gone.

I don't know if it was some antibiotic or something he got, but whatever it was, I want some of that. It has been bugging me since the end of 2016. I thought it would go away, but here we are, and I am still talking about it. If you have had anything similar for a long time, then you know.

Finally, I spent the better part of the last 18 months listening to all the advice given to us about

COVID-19. I knew from the get-go, before the weird interruption of an NBA game that caused us all to learn about it together in March 2020, that it was going to be bad. Did I think that it was going to be 700,000 dead bad? No, not at all. A lot of people don't realize that 700,000 people are the size of El Paso, Texas. It's the size of Denver. It's the size of DC. It's an insane amount of people, and even if you are one of the weirdos that think COVID-19 didn't kill all those people, that doctors "listed everyone as dying of COVID-19" or whatever, I got two things to say to you.

First of all, please shut the hell up. Secondly, even if it's 0.5% of what "THEY" say, that's still 3,000 people that died, which is as many people as 9/11. So, I don't want to hear COVID-19 talk from ignorant people, especially since I mentioned this.

On the last day of August, I was diagnosed with COVID-19. How the hell did I make it a year and a half successfully avoiding it, only for it to get me finally? How do you ask? I went to stupid Las Vegas for a weekend with my brother.

Ahh, Las Vegas, my second home and a place I love so much, I wrote two books under a pseudonym about my crazy times in my 20s in Vegas. I can romanticize even the rancid sewage smell that is under a vent just outside of Flamingo as an "Ahhh. I'm in Vegas" moment. I spent my adult life learning all the tricks, coupons, and things the average person doesn't know about Vegas.

I learned one thing early on as well. I get sick all the time when coming back from Vegas. Colds were regular. Flu happened once or twice. I had this crazy illness on Christmas Day 2018 that sidelined me for a month. The only thing worse than that was I believe I got was COVID-19 in August.

This trip was sprung on me with two days' notice, and I spent less than $100 the whole weekend. It was my first trip to Vegas since 2019, and obviously, the first time since the virus entered our lives. I wanted to visually document "COVID" Vegas and tell stories to my wife, who had to work. I was cautious with hand sanitizer, and masks were required, even at Allegiant Stadium, where we went to see WWE Summerslam. It was a bucket list event that nearly made me kick the bucket

Ironically, I posted to my Facebook friends that I attended my "first super-spreader event in 2 years" in Vegas. I meant it to be a little funny. I regret ever freaking saying that. Idiot...

I got home that Sunday night, after two 11-hour drives in 48 hours to total exhaustion. I slept for ten hours, and I didn't feel right. I had a problem, though. I was going to a concert with my brother and niece in El Paso two days later. I was going to see Megadeth and Lamb of God. Typically metal concerts drive up to my adrenaline. Dude, I felt like an old man after walking around 10 hours at Disneyland. I was so tired and weak. I just chalked it up to Vegas hangover. I didn't drink, but that's what I call being back home exhausted after a busy Vegas weekend.

That car ride back from El Paso, only 40 minutes in length, felt longer than the 11 hours from Vegas. Something was wrong. It wasn't until I told my wife goodnight before she went to bed the next night that I felt something crazy. I felt like I was on fire. The burning also made my muscles cramp and hurt. I was having restless legs and breathing weirdly when my wife said, "What the hell is wrong with you?"

Usually finding a funny rejoinder to come back with, it wasn't happening this time. I just said, "I feel like I'm on fire."

She tells me to check my temperature. 102.8 degrees. What the fuck?!?! I was stunned. I was banished to the guest room for the night. I was sitting there feeling like a sausage cooking in the oven. About an hour later, I was cold, and I had to pull a hoodie out of the closet and bundle up when I went to bed. I checked my temperature an hour later. I was at 96.0 degrees! I finally fell asleep.

I woke up in a pool of sweat. No exaggeration, it was the most I have ever seen myself sweat, and I am both a gym rat and once spent a summer day in Needles, California. It was no ordinary sweat. It was beyond what you would get in a heavy workout. It was viscous, and it smelled. How can your body do such things?

I felt normal that Thursday morning and did my usual routine on social media, but then I got those hot flashes again. My temperature was reading 102.0 now! I retired to bed at 6:45 pm, one of the earliest times I ever went to bed. I slept for 14 hours, interrupting my sleep to put on a hoodie again because I ended up with chills again.

To say I was prepared for quarantine was an enormous understatement. As an extreme couponer, I had food for the zombie apocalypse. It just sucked being in what was my jail cell for nearly three weeks. That next day, my wife bought an at-home testing kit. It was positive, and then I wanted to make it official, so I went to an on-site testing location, and sure enough, it confirmed it.

Test Result:

POSITIVE

Test Type
COVID-19 RT-qPCR test

Patient:
Baca, James

Appointment window:
09/01/2021, 8:30 AM - 9:00 AM MDT

Site:
DACC
2800 N Sonoma Ranch BLVD Las Cruces, NM 88011

Lab:
Curative San Dimas

I lost 18 pounds in 10 days. I don't care how goddamn big I am. 18 pounds is a Thanksgiving turkey. Yes, I was fully vaccinated the first week I was allowed to get it for those of you wondering.

Here's the thing, though. On my 5th day, stuck in that room, after another night of alternating fever and chills, I was having a hard time breathing while lying down. Although I think I have a sleep disorder as well (I forgot that I wanted to get that checked), it was the first time I was awake, laying down, and feeling how hard it was to breathe in bed.

This was before the health insurance I bought was to kick in. I thought about it. What if I needed to be in the hospital before it kicked in? I would be financially ruined. I would have a six-figure hospital bill that would follow me until the day I die. I have helped many people with mortgages and bills from twenty years ago and medical bills still follow them. Never believe that "it drops off your credit after seven years" shit. Trust me. It carries on forever.

It got me so upset because there are people in this same boat. A trip to the emergency room is the equivalent of buying a car if you have no health insurance. I am either blessed or cursed. It depends on how you look at it. By the fact I think of money almost every second of every day. That's the bank training, coupled with the close confidante status I have with so many people. The money would have influenced whether I lived or died had I needed to be hospitalized with COVID-19. I probably would have lied to my wife about not breathing well and probably pass away in my sleep.

For the record, yes, she got COVID-19 as well, and she had a much easier time with it. I felt so guilty that she got it because of my selfish trip to Vegas.

I do feel a lot better one month removed from having COVID-19. The weight hasn't come back, and I feel out of breath a lot easier than usual, but other than that, I was glad to be able to do the things I love again. But the way I see it is that I realized that my supposed "great health" is not true, as it is for many people in self-denial.

New Mexico Department of Workforce Solutions failed me in this sense. I can never get this fantastic opportunity back, even if I get approved immediately. My three-month window of health insurance will expire at year's end, and next year, healthcare will cost me $4,000 for insurance out of pocket, not including deductibles, co-pays, and medicine. It's like getting elbowed in the face for a TV at Black Friday. Did you choose to hurt me and hurt others over a few thousand bucks?

Even if you doubled my money, you idiots, you can't turn back time, and that's the shit I resent the most.

Mental Health

Boy, you want to talk about uncomfy. Wait until you read this part. I mentioned I lost five customers I helped at the bank that I was close with over the years to suicide. I lost a close friend in 2016 to suicide, and I have spent the better part of my adult life coming to grips with being an emotional person. I think a lot of people that don't have battles with mental health cannot comprehend how one feels whenever one feels so low.

Fighting with NMDWS has taken me to a low place I hadn't felt in three years, and funny enough, it's a selfish thing to me. I help so many people with banks and see how they treat specific individuals, and it doesn't affect me mentally, but when someone turns the tables on me, it feels like everything is that much more of a travesty. I guess because it's ME, you know? Selfish James.

There's always challenges with your emotions every step of life. It doesn't differ for anyone, but the way people can handle it varies greatly. Recently, I have taken some serious shots to the psyche, that I am writing this to make it abundantly clear that I resent my home state for being shit on Unemployment.

I would have LOVED to have used some of this backdated unemployment claim, coupled with the health insurance claims, of course, to have some face-to-face therapy. I am not talking about throwing a straitjacket on me and sending me to a rubber room. I just need a little… 30,000-mile checkup of the ol' noggin. That's all.

I am blessed with a wife I can talk to about anything, including the most uncomfortable conversations. She is not a specialist, though, and of course, through the prism of marriage, she is my wife, and by legal standing, she has a bias in favor of me. It's hard to work through problems with a person who doesn't have to be objective.

Without question, people don't talk about mental health enough, and frankly, people of color, like me, don't do it as well. I was always seen as emo and soft because I wanted to talk out things instead of beating up people. I was seen as a snitch when I tried to stop a harasser from bugging my family and me. The world is cutthroat, but I didn't know that I did anything to draw knives from people, you know?

There are three seminal moments in the last four years that have defined stress, anxiety, and depression on another level for me, and frankly, I want to deal with them so I can move on with my life. All three are technically intertwined in a way.

In 2017, my twin nieces were born prematurely. They were only at 23 weeks when they were going to be brought into the world. I remember that night, being on a high at the football stadium where the home team won, only to be brought into reality in a brusque manner. I was told we were going to my brother's house because they were heading to the hospital for an emergency. We were assigned the duty to take care of my niece, who was sleeping in her bedroom.

My wife and I were asleep on the couch when we were awakened the following day by the news that my two nieces, Briella and Ariya were born. It was a moment that was supposed to be joyful, but the sight of the calendar and the distant expectation of a due date told us that it was anything but a moment to celebrate. We didn't know if the girls were going to make it.

It was hard to comprehend because you had a vision in your head about two awesome little girls climbing Uncle James, swinging on his arms, having marshmallow eating contests like the other nieces and nephews I had and have had since. You knew that best-case scenario, you would be lucky to be graced by their presence at all.

That Sunday was a bizarre day. We went to the WWE show in town as a means of distraction, but I mean, who can NOT be focused on those girls in NICU. I attended the event, but my mind was elsewhere. The following day at the bank was the same feeling. Not knowing the result of what was going to happen was hurting me inside.

Monday night, over dinner, my wife Gabrielle tells me that they don't think Briella will make it beyond that night. It was a thud right in my gut. I didn't immediately cry, but I was understandably somber. I was going to have to say goodbye to someone I never said hello to.

Knowing that my mom was making her way down here made it more than official that Briella would get her angel wings. The day was going to be planned around food and family, and of course, they wanted Uncle James there to mourn as well.

I had to do one thing first. I had to go to work on Tuesday morning to inform my manager of the death in the family and to let them know I would be gone for at least one day. This would be the first personal day I had taken since 2006, an entire decade earlier, when my grandpa died. You kind of figure asking for a day off is pretty ceremonial when people die, right?

You need to understand that I adored my coworkers while I had a love/hate relationship working at Bank of America. They were the reason that made shit bearable at times over the years. I wanted to let my work family know why I couldn't be with them on a random Tuesday in September. I thought it would be in-and-out, ten minutes tops.

Went into work fully dressed in a suit. I just felt it appropriate to be within the dress code, despite likely not being there for too long. My friend, Stacie, a teller, already knew what was going on, as she was a friend outside of work. So, I made it over to Barbie, my branch manager, and I told her what had happened and what I needed to do.

In a very characteristic manner of speaking for her, which is usually not bad in my opinion, but it certainly was here, she curtly said, "You got to call Maria for this. Get her on the phone."

Maria was my market executive, which was the boss of the bankers and branch managers. There was a hierarchy change the year before that you had to report to her if you were sick or needing to take a personal day. I never called in nor needed personal days before, so it was all virgin territory for me.

I called Maria up, and I told her that I needed a personal day. I told her about my niece dying, but I don't know if she heard me and ignored me or didn't comprehend what I said, but she said to me, "James, you know we really can't be taking a personal day at the end of the quarter. Your location and you are so close to funding. I have to question your commitment by asking for this day off."

So, a couple of things to clean up here. This day was September 26, 2017. We were four days away from the end of the 3rd quarter of the year. BofA does sales goals by quarter. My branch was not at 100% yet, nor was I. You must be at 100% of your goal even to be considered for your quarterly bonus. Missing work put me, my manager, and Maria, my market exec, at risk of losing money by not hitting our goal.

I was called out for asking off this day because of money. Money that would be made by overselling customers. I freaked out. I had seen the bank's true colors many times before, but this one was cold. Prioritizing opening a few accounts over my deceased niece was too much. I freaked out. I never had anything resembling a panic attack until that moment.

Barbie told me to just sit in the back after I hung up the phone. I was in no condition to help customers. It was a surreal experience. A dead 2-day old baby was less critical than the checking accounts I generated. Every bit of desire to become CEO or even regional manager went up in flames that day.

I tried calling Maria again an hour later, and I got a voicemail. A few minutes later, I got an email from Maria.

"Is there an emergency or something that can't wait until I am done with the sales meeting? I will be done at 11."

Two more hours of being isolated in some break room while my family expected my presence seemed like two days. It wasn't until Stacie saw me in the back, a jittery, crying mess, that I got an email about twenty minutes later that said, "Condolences to you and your family. Go be there with them." from Maria. Stacie or Barbie must have gone to bat for me to get me out of there.

The damage had been done, though. I had to stop at a Dairy Queen on the way to my brother's house, and I spent $15 on ice cream. I ate it in minutes, and I went home and cried and dipped into some vodka instead of being with my family. I was in no mood to be the one consoling them. I have spent every day since then not having sympathy for corporate world coldness. My advocacy project always has its pilot light lit by that moment, and for every branch with a sales goal, there are people in the banking industry and their clients that are collateral damage for their revenue.

Secondly, most recently, in May 2021, I lost my other niece, Ariya, after living 3.5 years of an amazing life. She was born with many challenges. She would never say her first words, see or walk for herself, but she inspired other people and me with her amazing strength. When her sister passed, I got to see Ariya in an incubator. She was no wider than my wrist. She weighed less than a pound.

Months later, she finally got to go home, and she became my buddy for the rest of her days. The smiles she would crack and the grip she would have on your fingers as she held your hand were things that you can't ever forget about. I loved that little girl so so much.

The week before Memorial Day in 2021, my wife Gabrielle and I went to visit my brother and his family for the evening. They live a couple of miles from me. Conversation, food, and board games were on deck that night. Mainly, I wanted to hold my niece. She was getting so big, her head, once totally bald, now had a shock of beautiful long hair. I held her in my arms like she was a baby still. For a couple of hours, I got to rub her back, and I whispered "I love you" about 32893 times to her. It was soothing for me, as I hope it was for her.

My advocacy work makes me have to experience negative things with many people, so this peaceful night was needed to balance me out. Little did I know that this would be the last time I got to hold her in my arms. The next day, she got sick enough to fly from NM to Phoenix, AZ, and five days later, we made the journey to Arizona, kind of knowing this would be goodbye but praying that it wouldn't be.

She passed away Sunday, May 30, 2021, after 3.5 years of toughness and grace. I was devastated, as was my whole family, of course. The battle that Ariya had along with her sister is forever intertwined in my determination to help people because their births allowed me to see the important things in life and see many things I want to change about our priorities as a society.

I will love you forever, my cutie pie!

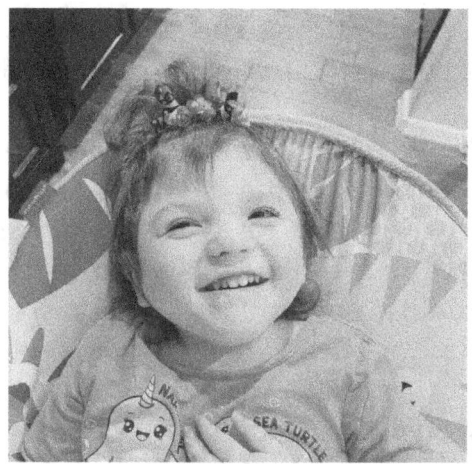

This event added to my mental plate because I stayed in a hotel suite with my brother, sister-in-law, my other niece, her friend, my mom, my aunt, and my wife. The lack of funds in my bank account, precipitated by waiting for NMDWS to fix my unemployment, played a part in being on the cheap at that moment.

If I had MY money, I would have been able to get a room for everyone not in my brother's immediate family to give them the peace and mourning time they need. Instead, it resembled the opening scenes of "Home Alone." I'll never forgive NMDWS for that. There's no "sorry" they can offer to alter that moment.

Grieving is terrible enough. Dealing with the stress and overcoming depression has been a lot in my life. Being a high-strung kid, introduced to a lot of the world's problems through my mom's eyes, my schooling, and my career has made me a head case. It's not PC to call it that, but I know that mentally, it's been a crazy ride the last 38 years.

One of the things I have had to deal with recently, which is CRAZY to me that it's still happening, is bullying. Let me be totally clear here. I was bullied as a kid, in high school, my supposed "best friends" bullied me, and even at 38 freakin' years old, I am getting bullied by the same damn people I can't shake. I guess I should call it harassment because I am not even engaging with these people.

My bully is the transportation director for the City of Socorro. His name is Carlos Savedra. He holds a government job, and he is constantly harassing my family and me on social media. Whether it's mocking my weight, sexuality, my job loss a few years ago, and the advocacy project I do now, it's always something with him. At first, I tried to defend myself, but it only got worse. I reported him for bullying on Facebook.

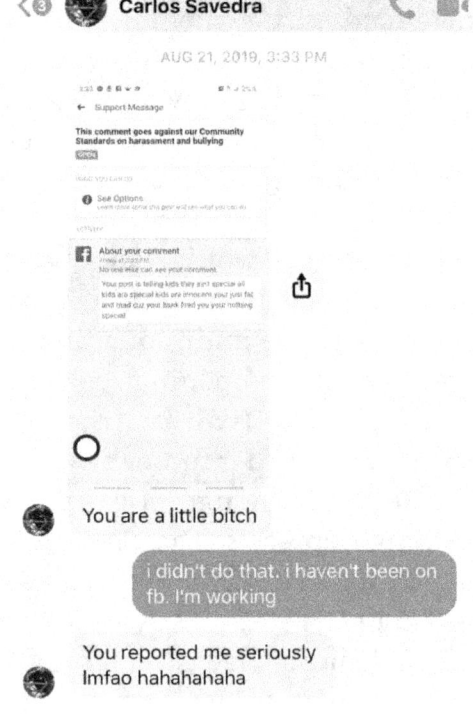

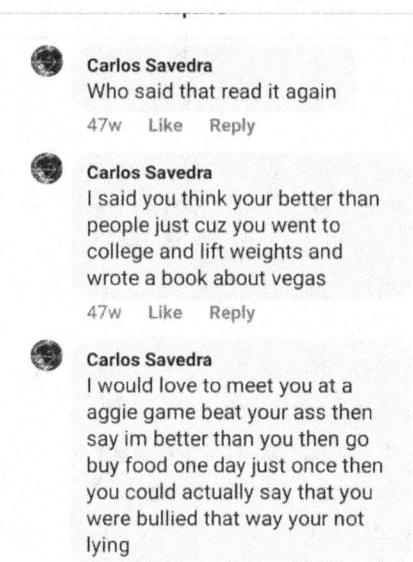

It all finally came to a head last year, when he was calling me incessantly on Facebook messenger while on the clock at his job and threatening violence on me and my family. For what? I don't know. I finally had to do something. I filed a police report, and I reported the harassment to his boss, a man by the name of Donald Monette. I sent him every piece of harassment I got from him with timestamps that indicated he did this while at work and told him that I had filed a police report.

Because a lot of the harassment happened in my public advocacy channels, I had somewhere in the neighborhood of fifty people reach out to Monette on my behalf, indicating the harassment, as Carlos put his name and job title out there for the world to see.

Several city council members including Michael Olguin, Jr., who I knew from the bank were involved in reviewing the data I and others had presented. Two days later, I got an email from Monette. He claims that I was harassing Carlos and that he gave him "a talking to." He blamed ME for Carlos harassing me. That's typical Socorro home-cookin'. The stench of local New Mexico politics and good ol' boy networks stunk that day. It sent me into a month-long tailspin where I couldn't function, much less help anyone.

I share all of this with earnest hope that a conversation on bullying can come up. You have people who work for a city, ENTRUSTED in the responsibilities of a community like Mr. Savedra and Mr. Monette are. You then have one person who makes it his regular duty to put me, my family, and my work down, and another person, his supervisor who looks to blame anyone but the person in front of him. That's what I need to know all about my local and state government in a nutshell.

You may wonder why I even mention this as part of this book? Well, it has amplified my depression a tremendous amount, of course. But mainly, the reason I say it was a few weeks ago, I woke up to a cacophony of laughing emojis on my Facebook from Carlos, who was using a second Facebook account, ironically with his name on it. He was laughing at almost anything introspective and honest I did. One thing crossed the line, though. He laughed at the announcement and memorial of my niece Ariya who passed away in May.

I have tried hard to hide this emotion from everyone, and except for a couple of times I raised my voice, I have done an excellent job. I haven't materialized it into words until writing it right now. I know that writing it is helping, but a conversation with a professional would be much better.

I am outlining all this stuff to show that this money was long spent in my head to do things to better my life, and the state has only made it worse, dragging it on like this.

So basically, Medical Insurance was the main thing I wanted to get with this unemployment money. While I have the card, I can't capitalize on it as much as I wanted because of this malaise that NMDWS has put on my application. Everything I mentioned I needed to be done would significantly improve my quality of life to function as an amazing cog in society's machine. Because the state has failed in every aspect to address my concerns, that cog is busted.

I want to get right again, physically and mentally.

Author's Note: I have talked about depression a lot with my project, and how my past work experiences, and other life experiences have caused these issues. I am not afraid to discuss these things with anyone, nor should YOU. Unemployment, COVID-19, anything that can impact you can hurt you mentally, but DO know that it's ok not to be ok. If you ever need someone to talk to, I am here, or you can call the National Suicide Prevention Hotline at 1-800-273-TALK.

I may not be able to solve problems, but I am a good listener. Just want people to listen to me once and hope that my story can help others!

Student Loan Debt

I know what you are thinking. Boo-hoo. We all got student loan debt. I know. I get it. Join the club, James. Student loan debt is the bane of a lot of people's existence. Collectively, America owes $1.6 Trillion. That's a million dollars multiplied 1.6 million times! Let me write in numerical form. $1,600,000,000,000.00. That's a fuckton of money. I always wanted to write fuckton in a book! Now I did it twice.

When I went to an alternative high school, the "Real" high school did something shitty. They refused to let us go onto the main Socorro High School campus for guidance counseling, saying that "Occasionally, we will send the counselors to your campus." That never happened. A couple of times, they sent a bunch of pamphlets on FAFSA and standardized testing but never actually went to help the people who wanted to go to school reach that goal.

Whether or not they thought the teen moms, juvenile delinquents, or just plain slackers like me were going to go to college or not, they didn't even go through the motions to help. It took me years to realize how much they did a disservice to the kids there with me the last three years of school I attended there.

No counselors to teach us about planning for college, financial aid, or anything that we didn't know about because most of my classmates' parents didn't know shit either. I might have been more motivated to go to school immediately after high school if I had those people entrusted to help kids like me get access to us instead of labeling my whole alternative school a bunch of cast-offs. I am pretty confident that I am the only person in that school to graduate from college. I racked my brain hard and couldn't think of one person at all.

But who cares, right? It was 20 years ago. Well, the fucking student loan debt is real today. Yep, I get an email every 13th of the month telling me about a scheduled payment for my loans coming out a couple of days later. It's only $50, but it's still a reminder of the shitty school district I attended high school at and the lack of knowledge I had taking out loans in my 20s. It's no one's fault but my own, I get that.

One of the cool things about working in banking was making decent enough money to let $200 a check go to loans, and I did that for eight years until I left. I whittled down $20,000 in student loans to a pretty remarkable number.

I owe $558.01 as of the writing of this book. That's amazing to me. This means in 12 more payments, this sonofabitch is gone forever. But ten months ago, when I owed closer to $1100, I had a thought. "Hey, when I get my unemployment, I am just going to pay this to $0 and be done with it." The reason being, if I just took care of it, It opened up $50 in my monthly budget, which honestly can be used for so many things. You don't know the power of $50 until you have it available to you.

This is what my financial training taught me to do. Budgets are everything. Because of this delay in getting my unemployment, I am halfway to paying off the remaining student debt. Still, I can tell you that this was a genuine intention of mine, as this fucking student loan has impacted my credit, my buying power, and honestly, anchored me to a stressful life for a decade.

Part of what motivated me to talk about what I intended to do with my unemployment money was seeing a piece on "60 Minutes" on how military members were sold a bill of goods about their student loans. Many weird things happened, and not only were the loans not forgiven as promised, but the military members were also told that the public service life they were required to have counted toward $0 off their tab. They owed everything in full.

Crazy requests, long hold times, and confusing paperwork, even for the skilled lawyers in that story, caused issues that led to them getting screwed over. Sound familiar? I think I have written something similar about me. That's the way it is, though. People who think they are more intelligent than you always try to one-up you, and it takes someone to speak up to facilitate change. Sound familiar?

Because of you dragging your feet, NMDWS, I am not going to be able to pay off my loan balance immediately, and the company holding my loans will make a few more bucks after making thousands taking advantage of a naive James a decade and a half ago. Thank You.

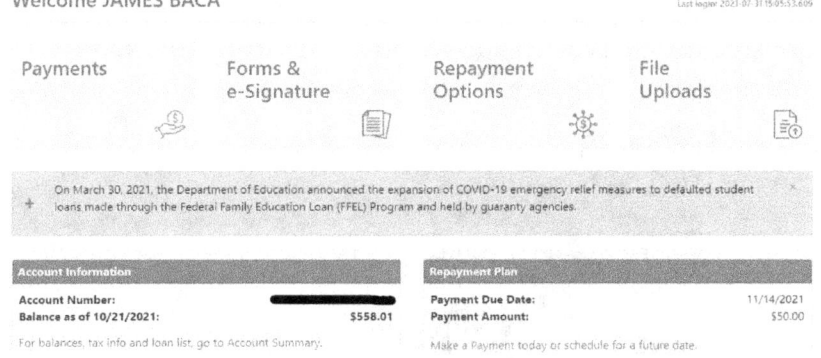

High-End Car Battery

Ok, James, your "wish list" of things that you were planning to do with your money is getting a little weird. Why the hell are you talking about a car battery, much less a "high-end" one? Things can get weird with me, but this one is seemingly practical. I guess I can say that I want a new car, but the reality is here. The money owed to me by NMDWS is not enough to buy a decent new car or even an amazing used one. It's enough to allow me to get by with my POS car.

I grew up with a dad who thinks about cars the way I do about cars. I don't use cars as a fashion statement or something to accent my personality. I don't "trick" out my cars, nor do I spend $15 on a premium car wash for it. I treat my cars as the thing to get me to where I need to go in town. Period. I just want the fucking thing to work to get my chicken nuggets.

James Baca is the proud owner of a 2006 Jeep Liberty with 204,000 miles. I love it. I loved my Explorer before that. It was a 2000 model. I bought both to get me to work and back. Since I am at home, like so many new remote workers, I don't need it for the commute, just basic tasks. No more, no less. My wife and I would use a rental car for a long-distance trip anyway, so having an old car doesn't impact vacations when I can afford them.

My Explorer didn't have power anything in it. It didn't even have a tilt wheel. Note to self: Never talk shit about a car ad that advertises tilt wheel as a feature. It sucks without it. This Jeep did, but when I paid $3800 cash for it years ago, it had something wrong with it that I didn't know about it. Well, two things. One, it burns off oil, which means I got to feed it every couple of months or so, and secondly, it has a parasitic draw, among other electrical issues.

So the dome lights never worked, and the power windows aren't great, but the shittiest thing about that damn car is the parasitic draw. For those of you who don't know what that is, it's your car just WASTING energy from the battery, even when it is just sitting there. Jeep message boards have speculated that it is likely from the car alarm or something with the fuses. I have tried everything.

I went through 3 batteries in the last five years. I used to buy el cheapo Walmart specials, called valu-start or something to that effect for my explorer, and it would take years to die. This parasitic draw eats valu-start batteries for breakfast. Within days, it killed that battery, and that battery couldn't be recharged!

I assumed it was a bad battery and a faulty cell or something, but I decided to upgrade and buy the top-shelf battery. Yes, Walmart treats their batteries like a high-end bar treats liquor. I purchased the Maker's Mark Bourbon of batteries after years of buying Ol' Grandad. I spent maybe $140 on the battery when I didn't have much money a few years ago.

I plugged that baby in, and my car was strong as an ox. It sounded amazing. But through the sometimes freezing desert winter nights, the Makers Mark battery loses its juice. What once sounded like a high-end car cranking over now sounds like a low-testosterone middle-aged man grunting his way through a crappy morning before having his coffee. What the hell is going on?

Unfortunately, I became a Karen at that moment, and I went to Walmart not even a year after buying it and telling them this battery is pure shit. I was livid, mainly because I am not one to buy the most expensive version of something. I am a cheapskate, as if you didn't know this by now. I didn't need to go as crazy as I thought, as the battery has a 5-year warranty. It was still in the window of "free replacement." So I got another one from them, and lo and behold, it was having the same problem.

You don't know what this entails. Without starting it, I can't go more than 36 hours to charge it up, or it dies. Depending on the temperature outside, it can take less time. In the winter, to even give me a chance of not having to get it charged at AutoZone, I have to go on these scheduled late-evening 3-mile cruises around my neighborhood to charge it up. If my neighbors didn't know better, they'd think I was casing their house to steal their shit.

Don't worry, neighbors. NMDWS will not drive me to a life of crime.

Because identifying and fixing the parasitic draw can be costly, it will likely be too much to justify on an older car. The next best thing is to get a battery that I know will last me until my vehicle's dying breath, or at least close to it.

Half of America cannot afford a $400 emergency, and car repair falls into that. That's the world we live in, and that's how stretched thin these poor bastards are. I told my wife when I lost my job at BofA years ago that I have plenty of money to pay the bills for an extended period...unless I have a significant car repair. Then shit changes.

I think investing $250 on a high-end battery will be the way to get this done. The top of the line batteries at auto part stores don't even look like the batteries you are used to. They almost resemble a sleek toolbox instead of the big clunky black box you are used to. The "Cold-cranking amps" will overcome any cold day, and even with a parasitic draw, it will hold its own much longer than the top-shelf Walmart POS I bought.

Did I win you over yet? See, it's a practical item that will help me for years in the future! I don't think very many people understand the significance of this purchase for me. I am not going to buy rims or a stereo system. Hell, I am not even asking to fix the dome lights, I am merely wanting to know my car won't suck the life out of my battery overnight ever again!

Small Business Aspirations

I think the funniest thing about certifying for unemployment is the "job search requirements" that most states put you through. It was not a requirement for most of the first year of the pandemic for many reasons. First of all, many jobs that were once available were not during those crazy times in 2020. Some businesses were shut down. Even most states feel that putting job search requirements as steps to get certified for a weekly benefit was paying lip service to the process for no reason, that's why it went away.

There were moments in 2020, as there are moments now, that I was scared shitless about running out of money, so I did look for work outside my field, but not my realm. Though it was not required of me, per my backdated benefits request with NMDWS, I sent them a PDF file with all the companies I put in applications or interviewed for. Was I 10000% hell-bent on working for Verizon customer service or booking hotel rooms over the phone? Fuck, no, but this was the first time in my whole life that I thought, "I just have to get SOMETHING!"

The fact is, I overperformed on my requirements to show NMDWS that I deserved my back pay, and they still fucking denied me. Why did I overdo it? Because I know, much like the movie "Kingpin" taught me about the perception the "English" have with the Amish, you almost have to work twice as hard to get equal respect and prove superiority. Barely meeting the requirements for unemployment? That's for Quakers! Shout out to the 12 of you that will get that movie reference from 25 years ago.

I ran into a fabulously ridiculous yet familiar problem when I was trying to apply for some basic dead-end jobs for money. That being overeducated, over-skilled, and overqualified for a job is a thing. I have said many times before, I am not beneath a blue-collar job, Cleaning toilets isn't my thing, but it also doesn't bother me either. What BOTHERS me is a society that doesn't realize that it does have a caste system. When someone with a degree and managerial experience in banking at the highest level with a big company rolls into Jack in the Box to flip Jumbo Jacks, most managers will not hire that person. Why?

Because they know that it's a stepping stone to somewhere else. Do you think restaurants hire people knowing they have to do the bullshit hiring process again in 3 months? No, they don't. They are not stupid. They want reliability because in that world of working, you have to cover that shift yourself if you can't find someone reliable. That's why I never wanted to work as a GM in a motel.

I have had high-end clients at BofA from the hotel world, as the deposit runners were always the GMs. I also had a best friend who was a GM at a Staybridge Suites. They were always pissy people. Why? Because they had to work almost every weekend and every big holiday, because the night manager or the desk clerk would ALWAYS call in "sick" on the holiday, forcing them to do 14 hours bitterly on a day they wanted to have off.

Calling your shot shouldn't be something everyone gets to do because there would be chaos in the workforce. I admit that. But don't you think that the student loan debt incurred, the career I forged for 13 years, and the knowledge and work ethic it took to become what I was is not worth anything in a job search? NMDWS would likely say no. Fuck that, it should be worth something. Otherwise, why do anything?

Filling jobs isn't just about filling holes. It's about making sure filling that job is a fit for your workplace environment. Do you think Tom Brady won 7 Super

Bowls because New England and Tampa Bay signed Olympic gold medal sprinters as wide receivers and powerlifters who can squat 2000 pounds as his linemen? No, because at the end of the day, the sprinter might not be able to catch, the powerlifting lineman might be too buff and not flexible enough to properly defend Tom, and he would get killed. Trust me, I have met some powerlifters that were so buff, you wondered exactly how they wiped when they went to the restroom, but I digress.

No, Tom needed a big lumbering, yet wily 6'6" 280lb white dude to act as a giant bullseye at times when he needed to get some much-needed yards. Gronk, his favorite target for a decade, isn't the best player on that team; he's the BEST FIT! Those who know, know, and those people hold trophies at the end of the day.

My reintroduction to the workforce should be an excellent fit for all parties involved. That's why I have decided that I will actively look for something after I get my back pay, and then I will set up my small business properly that I have been dreaming of for three years.

So what does this have to do with money owed to me? I will get there. But the consumer advocacy that I have been doing for three years is a sustainable business, mainly because there will always be banks screwing over people. I am a trained, skilled fixer/crisis manager. I know how to address a bank problem better than anyone in polished black dress shoes at the moment.

I have done a lot of assistance for people with PPP loans, Fraud claims, and, yes, unemployment bullshit in other states in the last 18 months, all complimentary. But I have had communications with smaller banks about being a branded "fixer" of things/financial advisor and content creator. I got paid for a dry run at that in 2019 after my BofA unemployment stopped. It was cool.

While that's one part of what I want to do, I also have another element to my helping people better their financial lives. I don't want to disclose out loud what I will be doing for fear that someone will poach the idea before I file the proper legal paperwork, but I can tell you that this will benefit me and others, and frankly, the economy.

For LLC paperwork and all the requisite licenses, I will be using my backdated unemployment and pay the state some of the money back to get this Notorious Banker thing up and running legitimately.

I will also need to upgrade my computer. No, I won't be playing Call of Duty on it. I will be working. I can build a decent one myself for $200 and get a second monitor for maybe $75. I would upgrade my office studio with more green screens for content videos/conferencing. I will likely invest in better audio recording equipment for a series of how-to financial podcasts/audio I am thinking of doing.

Everything would cost $1000...maybe. I can make 100 times that if I do it right, and NMDWS can do things right for me for a change.

Clothing

I don't want to bore you to death. After all, I promised myself this would be a short book. I can find deals on "regular" clothes almost anytime. I am a muscle shirt and cargo shorts kind of guy usually. That is the direct result of 20-inch biceps and a bunch of narcissism when I was younger. There's a long-winded story I can tell you about how I got about $2500 in clothes simply by buying Pringles chips. I won't tell it here, but let's say I am good for "regular clothes" for years unless I get fat or skinny.

But to be professional, even with the remote working environment of my consumer advocacy project, The Notorious Banker, I need a nice suit that fits. No,

I am not getting custom Armani shit. I am not getting off the rack either. I am getting something that's at least a Tommy Hilfiger or comparable, 52 Regular, maybe an athletic fit coat, and some dress pants, 40-inch waists because I have big calves from lifting. I want a nice pair of dress shoes in case I need to meet people in person. 14EEEE is going to be hard to find, but I will, and could get them cheap.

I also have to buy some big and tall dress socks. Nothing fancy again, just something that doesn't cut off my circulation and makes my legs purple like when I was at BofA. There are some nice dress coats for $60-70 on Amazon, plus the pants are maybe half that price. Shoes? Maybe $50 if I get lucky. $150 to look like a million for work? Let's do it.

Other Things

Again, I am not a picky person, nor am I a greedy person. I can make money last a long, long time if I need to. That is an admirable trait. But sometimes, I want to load my baked potato, you know? That doesn't make me a bad person. For most of my day doing my consumer advocacy, I am in a tank top, like I am now. Does this infer because I work on this project from home that I am somehow lazy just because I am not wearing sleeves? Of course not.

I am not a weirdo that will drive 4 miles to save three cents on a gallon of gas, But I won't order a pizza at menu price. That's a self-defense mechanism. All I can say is this money that NMDWS owes will not be wasted one bit. I will preserve it like it was our last sip of water, and we are stuck in the middle of the desert.

Will I buy something Gummy or Gummi with the money? Yeah, but that's $1 out of $20,000+. Will I buy an alcoholic drink with it? No. Because I don't drink, smoke, or do drugs. I used to drink a little bit in my 20s, but it was not for me. Will I gamble? No, of course not. Despite my love for Vegas still, I have lost the gambling urge. I like to watch people and eat great food now...like an older person —no clubbing or craps table for me.

Will I pay for entertainment? Partially, yes. Although CNBC, Bloomberg, and Fox Business are part of my balanced breakfast for my project, I don't think it's terrible to have a DirecTV or a Netflix bill, even when you are on a fixed income. Everyone needs to decompress somehow. If watching "Chopped" is a crime, then lock me up right now.

I guess what I am saying here is, even if state governments made you print out an itemized list of shit you bought with money they gave you, I think my review would be clean. I believe the things that would be purchased with my unemployment money definitely should be bought anyway. Accountability is something that my state and many other states in the country don't have when it comes to money.

It has been my experience that many of the issues with state unemployment offices are in primarily blue states just as much as red states. While red-state governors and their administrations have, from day 1 of the pandemic, sought to cut off the necessary funds needed to stay afloat in these "unprecedented times," blue state governors, for the most part, had let the federal benefit remain until its expiration on September 4, 2021.

I am trying to say this is a very non-partisan way. The reason is this is how I function with my consumer advocacy project. The ones that claim to care the most about helping others (i.e., banks, state-run programs) tend to be the ones that drop the ball the hardest at times.

Republicans can be dickfaces and tell you that you don't need it, and at least...AT LEAST will not lead you on a goose chase, all the while publicly explaining that they will help you out. It's not in their nature, and I am OK with it. I prefer honesty and harshness over this phony stuff you see often. This is as far as you will ever see me be political. It's just not my style, but I call it as I see it.

California's Unemployment, otherwise known as EDD is engrossed with Bank of America, which I know very well. After all, I was propagandist-in-chief at my branch for years, because I was told to be. California is heavily blue, except for the "Governator" about 15 years ago. The sweetheart deal BofA had to do unemployment cards worked like a charm for them until 2020, when it all went to shit.

For the last year, both the state and the bank claimed that it was freezing the funds for victims of fraud and not releasing it to them right away, "For their protection". Give me a fucking break. It was for the protection of banks and the state, not eating losses with fraud that had accumulated with false claims. There are people on Twitter I first talked to about losing out on their unemployment money in April 2020 that are still waiting for money promised that will never come. I have seen letters the state sent them and the bullshit that BofA had sent them regarding the fraud on their cards. It's all phony empathy.

The state, the public, and even BofA were blaming non-chip debit cards as the reason for the fraud. My work will tell you that even if you have a chip card, it can still be used for fraudulent purposes. That's not good.

It's the state and in that case, the bank saying that you can't be trusted with this money, because WE think YOU lost the money, and if and when we find out you lost it, you will pay us back, or we will put a lien on your home or worse! That's dumb, but that's how this game works. NMDWS's website went from helpful little pop-ups helping you certify your benefits online to passive-aggressive threats of liens on your home, repayment, and criminal prosecution if you are doing fraud on the state.

Although I am sure 99.99999% of people who filed for benefits knew that, including ones that were committing fraud, and while I know you have to read disclosures at times, you don't have to do that there. The bank told me to read stuff verbatim for liability and ethical purposes. But I have a question to ask the State of New Mexico. Why do you have to be a bad cop when people are trying to certify their benefits? It looks like this:

"WE KNOW YOU'RE LYING. BY CLICKING THIS BUTTON, YOU ARE PROMISING THAT YOU AREN'T LYING, BECAUSE IF YOU CLICK ON IT AND YOU ARE, YOU ARE UP SHIT'S CREEK, AND YOU WILL HAVE TO GO TO PRISON IN LOS LUNAS, WHERE YOU WILL BE BEAT UP FOR THE COST OF TWO CIGARETTES BECAUSE YOUR CELLMATE THINKS YOU ARE A BITCH!"

I read those pop-ups, which started showing up a month before the federal benefits ended, and I said to myself, "Jesus, that was unnecessarily harsh!"

Of course, it didn't say what I said above, but it sure as shit felt like someone waving their dick around telling you that they can't wait to fucking bust you.

Bust what? I am just looking to pay my goddamn bills with money YOU owe ME.

I just showed you all that my heart and my wallet will be in the right place if the time comes that NMDWS ever gets their head out of their ass and pays me what they owe me. I promise you that my intentions will always be true, and I will use that money to help others through my project. You have my word. Maybe I should say it like an alert on the NMDWS website.

"I HONOR MY COMMITMENT TO YOU! IF I DON'T HONOR MY COMMITMENT TO YOU, AND YOU SEE I AM LYING, I EXPECT YOU TO FIND A BUNCH OF RATTLESNAKES, ANNOY THEM AND POINT THEM IN

PLEASE TRY YOUR CALL AGAIN LATER

MY DIRECTION!"

FINALLY...

I watched this documentary on HBO Max last night about public shaming called "15 Minutes of Shame", and it's about how the internet chews people up and spits them out when they feel they are assholes for doing something that pisses them off. It's a good watch. I recommend it.

There were a lot of lessons in that doc I already knew about social media and the internet as a whole because I have had the internet at my fingertips for a quarter-century. I have been part of good and evil on the internet, but now, I am exclusively good. I have grown up tremendously in the last few years.

That being said, I am afraid of how this book is received, mainly because I am so open about everything in my life. The reason I put the chapter talking to the person trained to think anyone asking for unemployment is fucking lazy is that I want to have authentic dialogues with people, even if they disagree on what I do.

At the end of the day, if I sell this book, regardless of what you think of it, and what I am asking the New Mexico Department of Workforce Solutions to do in remitting me money that I qualified for that I feel they owe me, you can't hate that this book BECAME the job. I sell 100 books; theoretically, that's $1000 in my pocket or 5% of what those idiots owe me, in my opinion.

I think America loves a good comeback, a good shaming, and a good middle finger f-you move, and I think this book is that all in one. To get people to listen, I have to bare my soul to you, which is my version of shaming. If I get the money by throwing this middle finger out there, the James comeback will begin. I am America!

I humorously write this book because I think travesties are so omnipresent in this world that claims to be working together that you can do nothing but laugh at how fucked it can be at times. I think you see the things that people go through, and you just sit there and go, "Ok, how in the hell can this be happening right now?" I think humor gets people to listen a lot more. I am not a PhD on this topic of unemployment, but my advocacy work, living through COVID-19, and work and life experience have made me an expert on how "they" (meaning people in a position of power) talk to us.

I wrote this whole thing in the time it took me to receive a denial of my claim and the two weeks I had to appeal my case. I thought for a split second that I was going to give up the fight, but then I thought of all the people I have run into in my life that gave up because the odds seemed insurmountable. They are not insurmountable here.

My thinking is that the people who were pressed into duty to judge everyone's appeal and everyone's backdated request for unemployment benefits were to look at them on a case-by-case basis. What happens with that, though, is the work always gets sloppy halfway through a herculean task like that. Even marathon runners can break down their mile splits in a race as proof that maintaining equal time and an equal pace is impossible because other elements factor into why numbers can differ throughout the race.

I feel that an individual sitting in some leather chair and a desk over 40 hours cannot possibly understand my story, nor can they know the stories of thousands of other people who feel like me. I think a lot of times, claims likely get denied because the person who is fighting the "System" cannot articulate precisely what is going on with them so that it will win the hard-ass person with the rubber stamp denial over.

All I am is fucking articulate. I have spent over a hundred pages telling you exactly what happened, how it happened, what's going to happen if my home state treats me this way and what I plan on doing to fight it. Nothing is ever succinct with this author. I will talk, and I will write to the point of exhaustion if something I am passionate about is in my purview.

Of course, I am passionate about MY MONEY.

October 15, 2021, I submitted my appeal to the state of New Mexico using an all-in-one printer my wife's grandma gave us. She never used it, and I just used it to scan my appeal, which could make my life exponentially better or possibly ruin it. I don't think she realized the significance of the gift at all. I do because it allowed me to submit and fax an appeal that's not as long as this book but long enough to get their attention at NMDWS.

If I didn't get this printer, I would have gone to the UPS Store to fax my appeal, and that would run $9. That is $9 I have, but $9 I shouldn't have to spend to hear my case about something that seems so slam dunk to approve, in my opinion. It's not even about the nine bucks. It's about all the mental cost. The fact of the matter is this: I'm exhausted from having to deal with NMDWS. I'm exhausted with having to fight for something that is only because of errors made by the system.

Working in banking, I saw a level of ignorance and narcissism by the highest regional executives as it pertained to our "needier" clients. We used to get reamed on not pushing them to the app because "the app has all the answers." Well, it didn't. It just had the answers to the questions the bank WANTED you to ask and not that you had that they saw as irrelevant. Many people who frequented the bank I worked at before it closed were concerned about their bank accounts and their ability to access them via the app. Why? Because the app wasn't working for them because their phones were out of date for BofA's app update.

So many clients of mine had what people lovingly referred to as Obamaphones. For those of you who have never consumed government cheese or had a caseworker have a file on you because you were seeking assistance for SOMETHING, you may not know about Obamaphones. (34) It was a program to get low-income people discounted cell phone service. If you qualified for the program, you were issued a pretty low-end smartphone, but the ability to connect to the wifi, of course, and call where you need to call.

It was a game-changer for a lot of people, and if you walk down main st. here in the city of Las Cruces, you will see a few homeless folks chilling in the plaza by the picnic tables with cell phones plugged into the outlets available out there, with some of them browsing the web on their phone. In a way, it's a cool notion, although I know some people freak out when they see transients. I am not one of them.

But there was one noticeable problem as I left in 2018. The low-end android smartphones that these poor souls had worked for a lot of things....except the Bank of America app. I have used this book to take many shots at my former company because one, they do it to themselves, and two, I got another book I have written about my time there. This is a fucked up valid shot, though. They update their app all the goddamn time for no good reason except to change the background color to a different shade. Weekly updates at times.

There are times that there is a major update to the app, and while that's fine to me because I am savvy enough to adapt to change, there was always a major problem with all these updates. It seemed like BofA would take major advantage of whatever features newer phones had, and in turn, make the app not supported on these lesser Obamaphones. You would get a prompt that your phone can no longer use the app. To me, this was dangerous for fixed-income people.

What do you tell a poor, fixed-income person with an Obamaphone that can't access the app you pushed them to as an alternative for real service?

"You're going to have to get a new phone!"

Fuck that. Even a mediocre phone now costs about $750, or about what a month of SSI is for many older people. You have effectively gotten rid of a problem and used their supposed "flaws" of being broke and voiceless against them. The messed up thing? After two successful logins to the app, BofA considers that person a "digital convert". If that person never looks at their account again, they will be lumped in with people who look ten times a day! It's a shame.

This is what I feel about this whole nationwide unemployment disaster. It's a carnival game, chock full of fixes to immediately eliminate many people from contention. I asked almost two years ago that I would prefer all my documents to come by mail from NMDWS. To this day, I still get nothing in the mail or by email. I have to fish around on the portal to see what's going on.

I always get a pop-up, "There's a new message in your "other" folder." I go to it, and there's nothing there. Was there supposed to be something there, or did you make a mistake, and you are sorry about it? What is this "other" message I supposedly have, and will it have a bearing on my claim since I can't get it?

I filed my appeal on October 15, 2021, and it took me an hour to fax it. No, not because of anything on my side. I was told by the company I paid money to fax my documents that the fax failed because "the line picked up" during faxing, which caused it to disconnect. I got refunded several times after several attempts of trying until it FINALLY went through. Say I went to a UPS store for this, and I tried it several times, and it never went through. Do you think the clerk would have given up? Probably.

Do I blame the state for that? Only slightly. I don't think someone was picking up the phone when my fax was calling the same way my stepdad used to get pissed at me for hogging the phone line with the internet connection in the 90s. The simple fact that I can't fucking appeal and send documents by email or web submission is another chink in the armor for me. Who has fax capability? What 20-something even knows how big the fax was back in the day?

I never learned how to use a fax machine until I worked at BofA, and every day online, I see tweets ridiculing BofA for still using faxing as a primary form of communication. The appeal form I have given online mentions an option to appeal online, but I have clicked through the damn thing a hundred times over. There is no option there.

Then I saw that NMDWS calls their appeal arm a "tribunal." New Mexico Department of Workforce Solutions has legit made filing for unemployment sound like Slobodan Milosevic is getting tried in The Hague, Netherlands, for war crimes. A tribunal? My visual association with "tribunal" is people in The Hague with large earpieces getting the translation of whoever is speaking at said trial. New Mexico, call it "The Appeals Department." Sometimes simple is better.

I wanted to mention this somewhere in the book, not as a means of kissing ass to the state or trying to make some noble statement about COVID-19 that you haven't heard people say a million times, no matter what side they are on. While I have my SEVERE issues with unemployment and a few other departments in the state,

I wanted to say one thing.

Though some would deem it heavy-handed and "tyrannical," I have no issues with how my state has handled the COVID-19 Pandemic as it pertains to masks and the capacity limits that plagued us all last year. Don't get me wrong, it fucking sucked. However, loving this state as much as I do, I am well aware of its problems, especially with health.

Let's face it. No one is healthy in New Mexico. We are primarily overweight, and we have a lot of smokers. We have a lot of alcoholism in this state. We have a lot of drug use in this state. I don't want to throw my mom under the bus as one of the smokers, but she is. I have never seen that woman drink a glass of water (WATER!!!) until she was 60, and she looked sick as a dog the day my niece died. It wasn't COVID-19, but my god, it was the first time I worried about this firebrand that was my mom.

I don't think if she got COVID-19, she would have had much of a chance. I can say that about everyone in my family older than me, including some 40-year old cousins. I am 38 and feel that my health, while not great, is significantly better than theirs, and that's why my COVID-19 wasn't more serious. I know that some people likely had their lives saved because of these extreme measures in my state. It was an inconvenience to many people, and we are still wearing masks until at least November 12, 2021, but I am content with how this has played out.

The shit thing for Governor Michelle Lujan Grisham and every governor in the US is that no matter what they did during the pandemic, it would be scrutinized whether they were heavy-handed or, in the case of a state like Texas, didn't give a fuck. We are a society that likes to point/counterpoint everything. I hate that part of society now. She would eat shit, become a meme, and be hated by the very people she was trying to help. It sucks, and I think COVID-19 killed my desire to ever run for public office.

I immediately changed the topic when I heard derogatory things about her or anyone who did what they could to mitigate COVID-19 because I didn't want to be a part of negativity. Let's get out of all this, and then we can rehash what we could have done better. Leaders elected should lead as they see fit, and we have an election every four years if you disagree. 'Merica.

This is where this book comes in. I don't for one second think the NMDWS is operating fine. I wouldn't hear the stories I have listened to, and I would not have the story I have told you if things were fine. How can I be denied unemployment for both "still working" and "lack of work" on the same sheet? Which is it? A more direct denial intelligently said to me might have swayed me from writing, but all I get is a busy signal and ghosting when I try to get help from anyone I see works for that department.

Ironically enough, my old assistant manager at BofA in my hometown works for this NMDWS now, and while I haven't talked to her in 8 years, I can tell you that since she worked for BofA, she is adept at dealing with bullshit. I know she knows how bad it can get in a workplace because we both worked for a toxic one before. I look forward to eventually talking to her when this is all over and telling her, "Man, you sure know how to pick companies to work for."

In closing, since this book costs money to print by the page, and I am losing more earnings with all my ranting, I just wanted to say that in the end, the only reason I decided to do this book was to help me, which in turn, helps others. If I write it, maybe a reporter in some fledgling newspaper would take notice of the deeper problems of NMDWS. Perhaps someone who got burned out of their money will be inspired to make a few phone calls and let people know that they were mistreated as well.

I grew up in a culture that didn't talk about real-world issues like unemployment, assistance, and they rarely had a public opinion about anything controversial. Social media has mutated this problem because we only talk behind a screen. You may read this book on a screen, but the words I wrote I firmly hope that if you or someone you know are dealing with similar issues, you don't go down without a fight. I can tell you from experience that when a bank says no, it usually doesn't mean that's the final word.

Keep pushing. Keep telling your story for yourself. For your family. For your state.

James Baca, the author of this book, has moments of clarity and nobility to make the world a better, more efficient place. But there are times, my homegrown instincts and cynicism get the best of me, and I will help light the match to stoke a flame of dissent when I say, "I don't believe you helped me or others to the best of your abilities." Or I can just go back to my "barrio" roots and say, "You are full of shit, bro."

State of New Mexico give me my damn money, please. Thank You.

BUT WAIT, THERE'S MORE!

It's funny. It always seems like the battles I have always have so many layers to them. I am the tiramisu of issues. For every idea of where something is going, other things divert my attention to something else I hadn't thought about yet. I am writing this chapter one chapter after basically saying "Goodbye" to you because I felt that October 15, 2021, was the day that I would appeal, and I would have a day to discuss my backdate unemployment request. Now, I write this on October 19, 2021, not knowing where my life will be at six weeks from now.

I purposefully will not try to rearrange my book to look pretty because what NMDWS threw at me as of last night was more than a monkey wrench; it was a whole fucking Sears Craftsman Tool Chest on wheels.

Note to self: Does anyone under 40 get the dated reference about Sears Department Stores, or am I just that old and out of touch?

I am going about my Monday night, which includes catching up on the over 100 emails I get daily from people to help with bank issues when I decide on a whim to see if NMDWS updated my appeal request for my unemployment benefits. I didn't know what I was expecting, but what I got was indeed something that I was not expecting.

Logging in, which by the way, was 100x more effortless than before, I noticed I had two pieces of correspondence waiting for me. I eagerly got to the inbox to see what it was. It was a letter setting my appeal hearing before the War Crimes Tribunal in The Hague… I mean the Appeals Tribunal in Albuquerque. It is listed for

December 6, 2021, which ironically enough is 16 years from the day my work career started at Bank of America. On that day in 2005, I wore a Walmart brand dress shirt and a clip-on tie, and the rest is bank history. The day before Pearl Harbor Day, 2021, might legitimately be the moment everything changes for me the way it did for this great country.

According to the document, the Tribunal will hear my case to answer the following questions:
"THE ISSUES TO BE HEARD DURING THE HEARING ARE: Whether the claimant has good cause to backdate the claim, pursuant to Section 51-1-5(A) and 11.3.300.301 NMAC. Section 51-1-38(H) Whether the claimant shall be liable to repay the Department all benefits received."

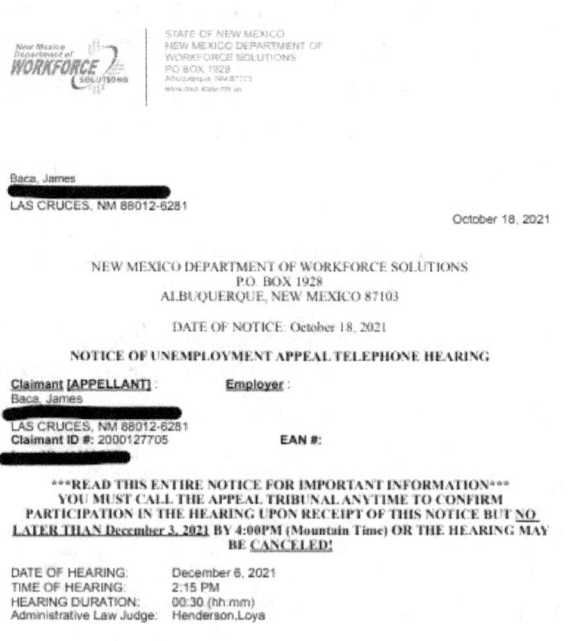

the hearing if you fail to confirm your participation in advance as instructed, even if you have previously provided a telephone number to the Department or confirmed participation for a previously scheduled hearing.

IF YOU MISS THE HEARING (REQUESTING A REOPENING): You must immediately submit a written request for reopening of the appeal explaining why you failed to participate at the hearing as instructed in this notice. If your request for reopening is not received within 15 calendar days from the date of the decision dismissing your appeal, your request to reopen the hearing may be denied.

RESCHEDULING: To ensure a prompt hearing, rescheduling requests are granted only for extenuating or extraordinary circumstances. You must submit a written request to reschedule that states specific details with attached supporting documentation as to the reason rescheduling is necessary. Unless you are advised the request is granted, you must call to confirm by 4:00PM on the date listed above. If you do not call a decision will be issued against you for your failure to confirm your participation.

THE ISSUES TO BE HEARD DURING THE HEARING ARE:

Whether the claimant has good cause to backdate the claim, pursuant to Section 51-1-5(A) and 11.3.300.301 NMAC.

Section 51-1-38(H)

Whether the claimant shall be liable to repay the Department all benefits received.

(Section references are to the New Mexico Unemployment Compensation Law NMSA 1978, and the New Mexico Administrative Code - Go to www.dws.state.nm.us for links to the full unemployment insurance rules). See the instructions on How to Prepare for Your Unemployment Insurance Appeal Hearing at www.dws.state.nm.us

INTERPRETER: If you do not speak English or are hearing impaired, let us know right away so that we can arrange an interpreter for you at no charge. Si usted no habla el buen inglés, avísenos inmediatamente que usted necesita un interprete. El Departamento le proveera un interprete gratuitamente.

CLAIMANT: If you are still unemployed, make sure you continue to file for benefits each week during the appeal process. Otherwise, you may not be paid for the weeks you are unemployed during the appeal process even if the appeal is decided in your favor. If you need assistance with filing weekly claims, contact the Claims Center at 1-877-NM-4MYUI (1-877-664-6984).

ADDRESS CHANGE: If you have an address change at any point after you have filed your appeal, you must notify the Appeals Tribunal in addition to the Claims Section (or Tax Section for employers) immediately.

IF YOU HAVE ADDITIONAL QUESTIONS ABOUT THE HEARING, call the Appeal Tribunal at 1-800-227-7325. If you have additional documents for the hearing you may fax them to (505) 841-8636. Please include Claimant Id or Employer EAN on all correspondence sent to NMDWS.

So, I'm not a lawyer, nor am I a genius and I didn't stay at a Holiday Inn Express either. I am just a college-educated person who worked at a bank. I had to learn the finer points about closing mortgages and procedures and policies to comply with all the regulatory bullshit that comes with banking. I also help people through complex solutions as a consumer advocate regularly. I may not know EVERYTHING, but I thought I knew enough to understand what was going on in this world. Can you riddle me this, Batman?

How the FUCK can we be having a meeting on two things that have absolutely NOTHING to do with each other? So, the first question asked is basically if I have reasonable cause to backdate my claim. My statement was that after trying over 1000+ phone calls, I could not get through to them for seven months, impeding my ability to speak to someone for help. When I put in the request, it was based on if I could have submitted my benefits application in December, and let's say I got denied at that point. IF I had been able to talk to someone, I would have never gotten money in the summer.

So, by that logic, how can the second question be "Whether the claimant shall be liable to repay the Department all benefits received?" Is it possible to have reasonable cause to backdate my claim AND be FORCED to repay something to the state of New Mexico? How does that make sense? Is question 2 irrelevant if I can show good cause, or is question 1 there for "decoration" sake to show that I would be getting a fair shake at appeal? How can both questions be reasonably answered?

Obviously, in July 2021, when I finally got through to a representative on the phone, Barry was the one who filled out my app, asked me questions, and walked me through the arduous process I had waited so long to do. Now that Barry is out of the fucking picture, why am I being held liable for information I submitted, and obviously, someone APPROVED that same week? I thought the whole review process for the application was done then? If they are only going to rubber-stamp it then and then call a foul on you later, why even do anything? Why would you put yourself in financial jeopardy?

The two question thing reminds me of the California Governor Recall Election of 2003 and 2021. Two questions are asked. (I'll paraphrase them)

    1. Do we kick the asshole governor out?

2. If yes, who do we pick to replace him?

Those questions at least go together.

My two questions have nothing to do with one another. It's like they are asking:
1. Did you prove to us that you qualified for the money from December 2020 to July 2021?
2. Do you need to pay the money back we approved from April 2020 to September 2021?

If I prove that I qualify, why is question 2 even a thing? From all of my time helping people through the claims process at BofA, I can tell you that this letter I got almost seems like it is there to scare you into dropping the appeal. If I didn't appeal my claim, it would seem like the repayment conversation would have never happened. But also, if I DID drop an appeal, would I get a letter in the mail one day, saying, "Pay us back, asshole!" without being able to fight it? Who knows?

Everything with gig workers and the self-employed was weird when the unemployment benefits thing came out last spring. I was even a bit skeptical of how things worked, but according to everything I read, I was in the clear. I earned income through my podcast sponsorships from the smaller banks who believed in me. I made money through contributions to my project through Patreon. I am the definition of self-employed. In a far-flung sense, you can see the podcast sponsorship being a "gig-worker" thing because a company paid me to promote them through social media and podcast media channels.

I didn't do anything wrong. I followed the instructions even though NMDWS instructions on all of this shit was worse than trying to put together IKEA Furniture on an acid trip. I never did acid, but I have many articles of IKEA furniture which my wife and I put together that turned into shouting matches because we didn't understand the instructions. Everything was done by the book with the materials given to me by the state.

The things that I did to apply? All done by reps for NMDWS. Much like a lot of my work with big banks, they are looking for a way to circumvent blame and put it on me without any legitimate excuse. Their claim is almost laughable in that they say that my inability to reach someone was no valid excuse and that when I did reach out to someone, the application that person took is now in question, and I might have to repay. What planet am I on?

Isn't the representative, the application they took, and the review of the checks and balances on my application part to validate my claim? Wasn't it safe to assume that I had a valid claim when I got money after talking to someone? Why are we ruling on things months later when the game is over?

This is like if Super Bowl LV was played in February. Tom Brady hoists up his 7th Lombardi Trophy. We get to the off-season, the NFL Draft, and then training camp rolls around, and all of a sudden, a meeting is held on Park Avenue in NYC (Where NFL HQ is) about the last season's Super Bowl.

It turns out Tom Brady forgot to date his contract that he signed with the Tampa Bay Buccaneers that past March, which invalidated that contract. His lawyers, the team's lawyers, and the NFL lawyers who handle the filing of player contracts all missed the missing date on his contract.

That July, a clerk in the NFL offices is tasked with moving all the year-old player contracts to the vault for safekeeping so the new contracts can be more accessible. She snoops at the first couple of contracts because don't we all like to snoop at things that aren't our business. She notices Tom Fucking Brady forgot to put 2020 or /20 or '20 on his contract where he signed.

As someone who had to redo a mortgage closing because of someone's missing date, that was a big no-no for Tom. The clerk tells her boss, "I dropped the contracts, and when I picked it up, I didn't want to look, and I saw that Tom didn't date his contract. Isn't that bad?"

The NFL middle manager goes, "Hmm. Interesting" Although he cannot show bias to any teams, the dude was born in Florissant, Missouri, and he has been a die-hard Chiefs fan since he was a kid. He is going to find a way to bring up this error to his boss, the commissioner. I wonder if this could be something terrible.

Commissioner sees the date missing on his contract. Because of the perceived bias that he had on the Patriots in 2014 during the deflating football scandal, he has been looking for a smoking gun to get one up on Brady, who famously didn't cooperate with him during that scandal. He takes it up with the owners of the teams. Because of the dislike towards New England and Brady during that time, the owners 23-8 to strip Tampa Bay of their Super Bowl. They will also make Tom Brady return the keys to the car he won, getting Super Bowl MVP and forcing Brady to pay back $25 Million because he neglected to date the contract.

Fucking far-fetched fan-fiction from a Cowboys fan there. HAHAHA. I used Tom Brady as an example TWICE in this book!

But I think you know what I am getting at. If Brady did not date his contract, and someone at the table said, "Hey, Tom, you forgot to date it, big man." Tom dates it, and we all share some pastries and coffee. The moral of that is if EVERYONE drops the ball, why does the onus fall where it did? Why is it on Brady when people are hired to see who "crossed the t's and dotted the i's"? Why would

I have to pay back the money when my file was reviewed several times, with no changes to it since the pandemic, given the green light to get money?

Although I believe I am right here, working in banking taught me one thing: That whole "bank error in your favor, collect $50" bullshit from the board game Monopoly is not real. No matter if someone fucked up, and there was tons of it during my process, they will punish you for their errors, or at least try.

My first ever podcast was about something similar. There was an ATM in a rough neighborhood of Houston that was spitting out $100 bills instead of $10 bills one night. It was a BofA ATM in a place that was ⅔ African-American by demographics. Knowing how much can fit in those ATMs, I can tell you at max capacity, it was $250k if it was all in $20 bills.

So, by that logic, there could have been $1.25 Million in that ATM that was put there incorrectly. The armored car people fill the ATMs, count it before putting it in, and document on a paper that they counted it correctly. So, a couple of people go to the ATM and notice the error, and they try again....OH, SHIT! IT'S GIVING US FREE MONEY!!!

People are only human, so word gets out, and hundreds of thousands are taken out that one crazy night in 2018. Police are summoned to the ATM because fights are breaking out. Chaos is ensuing. What is going on here?

The armored car person and the second person who didn't do their fucking job fucked up. They sign a paper saying, "Everything looks good." Now the bank, which contracted them to place that money, was out a lot of money, because of course, the armored car company is going to try to charge BofA for that mistake that they had nothing to do with. The police and Chief Art Acevedo of Houston, a man with a shady past regarding race relations, has a press conference that tells people to return the money, or you can face a felony grand theft charge.

We are in the middle of the Christmas season here. Bank of America, who, despite how horrible they can be, knows when they are in a no-win situation. Common sense says they should ask for the money back or deduct the difference from their bank account. They should have known.

But this is where the PR fucking machine comes in. I am sure the PR person at Bank of America said... "Do we want to steal money out of the accounts of mostly Black people during the holiday season because the armored car people didn't do their job correctly?"

Fuck that. Bank of America said in a statement that the people who got the extra money could keep the money, a move which still blows my fucking mind to this day. I once got yelled at for ordering paper for the printers at BofA. The paper was used to open accounts and give people required disclosures. You would have thought I bought a lap dance with the company card.

But they know that this is a losing battle, so these people get to keep the money. So, you got to see where I stand here. I am just good ol' James, sitting here, waiting for any response from NMDWS for SEVEN MONTHS. SEVEN MONTHS! I finally get help, and because of the shoddy job from the reps, I am now under scrutiny to possibly pay back some money.

Had my call been answered in the order that it was received, had I gotten the help that I and others deserved when we needed the help, I may never have been in this scenario and owed nothing because I got nothing.

Fixing mistakes is cool and all, but not at the expense of the people who needed your help, didn't give it to them, and when you did, you only hurt them more. Since I told my wife about this issue, she has told me stories about other people she knew who ran into some brick wall with NMDWS this year.

I talked to an old friend for the first time in 9 years today, and she told me that she knew people were forced to pay back some money. Did some people possibly not answer certain things truthfully? Of course! At the beginning of this book, I mentioned that I grew up with people who knew how to skirt the system, including my mom.

That doesn't mean everyone did. That doesn't mean I did. If I did anything I thought was untoward or incorrect, do you think I would write a fucking book? Shit, no. This isn't a James Bond villain who can't keep his mouth shut to James Bond about his master plan as he's trying to kill him. I would be incognito if I thought anything was not above board. I am a hard-working American and New Mexican who was paying into this system meant to help me and others and was invited by the federal government and the state to receive compensation because of COVID-19, based on my application and supporting documents. What exactly did I do wrong, Moneypenny?

(Sears jokes and James Bond references in one chapter. Not modern, James)

I now have to sit around like a dumbass for weeks with this cloud hanging over me that I might have to pay up to $20,000 back because someone decided that it was time to pick on old James. I can't afford that. I can't pay that. I will say right now that will be the knockout blow for me and that life will never be the same if they lay 2x the amount of debt on me that I already have.

I won't be able to function correctly until then as well, and honestly, who could? I feel like I am on trial for my life here. I then think of all the people they relegated into a life of high-interest car loans and renting shitty properties because they have this judgment on them.

Will these idiots put a lien on the house I live in? It's in my wife's name, and my name isn't even on the title, but will the ancient "Community-Property" bullshit that this state has impacted a woman who loves me and has stuck by me through these crazy times I have experienced?

You may notice I don't talk about her as much in this book. Why should I? She's an MBA with a great job and works hard for herself and our household. Why should she suffer because NMDWS refused to do their job correctly the first time? You are going to piss in her corn flakes because of some error you made with ME? How is that fair?

This is my battle, but she supports me in my case here because she knows I am on the right side here. If I had no battle to wage, she would talk me away from it.

There's no doubt that many of the households who will go through what I have to go through are not in a position to fight back and give up. They have kids and a lot of bills with not a lot of income. This would be their "unrealized value" if we talked like a bunch of fucking brokers here. I don't know how to articulate anymore how WRONG NMDWS has been for so many people, much less me since last year. You are ruining more lives than helping. While many people accept their fate, on principle, and because I see people get railroaded by large entities all the time, I can't take it. I will fight.

I think there are many things fucking broken with my state and the federal government besides this battle I am fighting. I get that, and I know I am not the only person in the world, so I know I don't deserve ALL the attention. I wouldn't say I like all the attention for this, a pretty embarrassing thing for someone to go through, to be honest. But some things need improving.

What's the point of help if you can't provide it promptly? Why are you going out of your way to prove people to be liars when all you wanted to do was help help help during the pandemic?

Because it never was about help, it was about the facade of help. You can help people on your timetable as long as you claim you are helping them. NMDWS is sending me and probably thousands of other people scary letters like this to "thin out the herd". I feel that the letter is sent out to scare you into withdrawing your appeal. They are giving you the incentive to quit the fight by saying you might owe us if your tribunal chief thinks you are full of shit.

Of course, with COVID-19 nearing the two-year mark of being in our lives, the attention is pushed away from subjects like the one I wrote a whole book on, and people are focusing on other things. There are a million stories like mine, although not many as quirky as mine. Those who are feeling what I feel might not have the words to express what a shit-show this has been. I'm not like those people.

I will tell you it's a shit-show, then write 60,000 words about why, and I will get my point across. This book was published before I knew my fate, but I will tell you this. They can't make me stop caring about other people. I plan on being on the side of anyone who needs my help articulating the plight. It is horrific to witness poor customer service and see my home state not give a shit if it frisbees people into deeper poverty. We in New Mexico know all about poverty.

Of course, New Mexico isn't California. This is a kiddie pool compared to the Olympic-Sized pool in Cali. You can still drown someone in a kiddie pool, though. It takes a certain callousness, but it can be done, and it is happening. New Mexico, I love you, but I need you to step away from the pool.

I still want my money.

PLEASE TRY YOUR CALL AGAIN LATER

Always fighting the good fight,
James A Baca

THANK YOU

I have written other books under pseudonyms, and I would always not take this "Thank You" page seriously as I am going to now. I would just add everyone's name in my life because no matter the role they played, if they influence the book in any way, I would include them. Call it a byproduct of always wanting to be included when I was younger.

That being said, I only have a few people to thank that are in my life for this book. I thank my amazing wife Gabrielle for the unconditional support she has given me as I sought meaning in my life after leaving banking. She believes in the work I do as The Notorious Banker, and she knows the stress this subject has put on me.

Of course, I want to thank myself, 38-year old James Baca, a person way different than he was fifteen years ago. I have matured, I have developed a conscience, and I seek to do good things for great people. Every word I type, every thought I think is genuine and has meaning these days. While I will not agree on everything you may believe in, I will give you the respect as a human that I, in turn, want as well. I did this book, so I can get help, but also allow the others impacted by similar situations to garner courage, confidence and determination to fight for what is theirs as well.

Thank you to Bank of America. Although the unethical sales practices and head games that management played on you to do the things they wanted caused me years of stress, I thank them for teaching me that "no" isn't always the final word in a conversation. If someone tells you "no", it's rarely the end, but an opportunity to learn what went wrong, and how to better your skills from that "no" that you got. I will someday write a book about Bank of America, and the skills they taught me will be used to amplify the things wrong with that company. But thank you for my persistence you instilled in me by force.

My mom, Cathy, showed me living proof of the saying, "It's not about the size of the dog in the fight, but the size of the fight in the dog." Although she probably will say, "What the fuck does that mean? Are you calling me a dog?" she has to know I have always respected her resilience not to let anyone push her around. Whether it's men, her workplace, or even the State of New Mexico when she refused child support checks she received a mere 30 years too late, she showed me never to take bullshit from anyone.

The author Shea Serrano, an inspiration to me in writing this. A fellow Mexican-American brother one state over. He gives back to others all the time, has a voice that is distinctively his, including shit-talking as needed, and is unapologetically himself.

Finally, as you can see, when I talk about serious topics, I try to sprinkle in humor in order to make sure you can laugh while getting educated on what I have to say. I have three comedians I admire that have given me the gift of "Hey, you can be angry, funny, and intelligent all at the same time," and those people are Bill Maher, Dennis Miller and the late George Carlin.

Maher for being unabashedly thought-provoking and politically incorrect, while being acerbically funny. Love him or hate him, he elicits a reaction from you. Dennis Miller, who I discovered at 14 years old. While I rarely agree with his current points-of-view, the fact of the matter is that I found my humor and ability to do monologues, such as I do on my podcasts and content videos by learning from his "rants." I am thankful for that, because without discovering his HBO show in the late 1990s, I'd have never found it.

Finally, George Carlin. The comedian who coined the "7 Dirty Words" bit that changed comedy. He was edgy before edgy was cool, and in some locales, legal. He never gave a shit, and he spent so much time perfecting the craft of talking to his audience. His humor inspired me in a lot of ways, but mainly to never believe what "they" are telling you.

When I was 17, I took a stand for something at my high school, in an age where post-Columbine, we had a lot of people poking into our school looking to change things which would have impacted my small alternative high school. I spoke up in person for the first time in my life, and got thrown out of school immediately for "insubordination". I then wrote an op-ed in my local newspaper calling out the school district for overstepping their power to my little school. The school called me, apologized, and did away with the proposed rule changes there. It was the most powerful feeling I ever felt, and I still feel it 21 years later.

I wrote to George in 2002, sent a copy of the op-ed I wrote, which looked and felt strikingly like his writing, minus the f-bombs, and a week later, he sent an autographed 8x10 and a personalized letter. It said, "James. Always Give Them Shit. George"
I will. Always.

Thank you all for reading!!!

ABOUT THE AUTHOR

James Baca Aka "The Notorious Banker"

My name is James Baca. I am in my late 30s, a self-described consumer advocate, mainly focusing on banks. I have 16 years of experience in the banking industry, with a healthy chunk of those years holding a managerial role at Bank of America.

Being a manager at Bank of America is the equivalent of being a member of the Colgate Cavity Patrol in that it's mostly a title to make the recipient of said title feel special that they are part of a club. The manager perks at BofA were long, tedious sales meetings, ass-chewings for not overselling your most loyal clients, fun side effects like weight gain and hair loss.

I was liberated from that job in 2018 when my company decided that being on the working-class side of my hometown, Las Cruces, NM was not economically viable for them. Since then, I have been a (primarily) volunteer consumer advocate for hire. I am known online as "The Notorious Banker."

I have extensive knowledge of customer service issues with my former company and other banks such as Wells Fargo, Chase, and Citi. I am effective at identifying problems for those who seek my help. I enjoy walking them through how to fix it with their bank effectively while identifying BS and lackluster service along the path to getting help.

In the three years since I have been charting my path, I have recovered close to $2 Million in fees incorrectly assessed by the major banks. I have also helped bank clients pursue fraud claims that their banks summarily ignored and even helped a couple of dozen people get through the horrible home loan hurdles banks put in front of clients they don't genuinely want to help. I also was lucky enough to help a couple of dozen businesses get through the PPP Loan process and paperwork with several banks.

I host a podcast called "The Notorious Banker," which points out consumer banking stories that clients should need to know about with a perspective only a cynical ex-banker can provide. I give uncensored commentary (I guess this is where I should mention there will be some adult language in this book) and perspective on how big banks are bad for America.

I conduct interviews with people who I've worked with, clients I have helped recover money for, and people charting their path financially despite hurdles along the way. I also give honest financial advice to people who seek it, and by that, I don't mean I give hot stock tips. I give advice that helps keep people afloat because, for the bulk of my 38 years, I have been either lower or lower-middle-class as it pertains to income.

I am a 2001 graduate of an Alternative High School in Socorro, NM called AIM High, where troublemakers go just to get their piece of paper and get a food-service job. I was the 4th ever high school graduate in my family, with my dad and uncles being the only three people to do so beforehand. I am also a 2008 graduate of Eastern New Mexico University with an associate degree, becoming the first person to graduate college in my family, with my brother doing so as well just three years later. I am a "Student of Life" (as some hippies call it) where I want to learn, and I want to experience so many things this world has to offer in the short time we have it.

Corporate America gave me a detour in my journey when I accepted a part-time teller job at Bank of America in Socorro, NM, in 2005. I continued there for three years until graduation, where I successfully transferred to a branch in Las Cruces, NM, as a "Head Teller" in September 2008, where I spent the next decade. I grew into various roles as Teller Supervisor, Vault Teller, Sales and Service Specialist, Personal Banker, and Relationship Manager, which is essentially the branch manager for sales.

I almost never missed a day of work and was regularly celebrated for my sales performance, which in hindsight was awarding me for overselling people stuff they didn't need. Being fired from the bank was likely the best thing that happened to me mentally and physically, as it took a toll on me. A second book will detail that journey at some point.
And now, I use my wealth of skills to help people in need, and hopefully, with the help of this book, help myself at the same time.

I have a wife, Gabrielle, and currently reside in Las Cruces, NM. No kids, no pets, just looking to help my fellow man. Hopefully this book helps people understand about what some are going through.

www.ingramcontent.com/pod-product-compliance
Lightning Source LLC
Chambersburg PA
CBHW052351220526
45465CB00003BA/1053